WHEN
SCIENCE
FAILS

When Science Fails

By

John Hudson Tiner

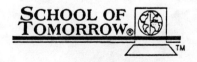

Accelerated Christian Education,® Inc.
Lewisville, Texas

Printed with permission by
ACCELERATED CHRISTIAN EDUCATION,° *INC.*

ISBN 1-56265-005-X

2 3 4 5 Printing/Year 95 94 93 92

Printed in the United States of America

Contents

TO JEANENE

Introduction

The number of cases in which science has failed is much higher than many people are prepared to believe.

A recent graduate course in astronomy reminded me of the unexpected errors that can still be found in science. The astronomy professor teaching the course had spent his life studying the solar system, and the textbook we used was a new edition by a recognized expert in the field.

The textbook described Mars as a planet with a rather uninteresting surface because of low gravity and high winds. Blowing sand would have worn mountains down to foothills, and valleys would be filled by drifting sand.

As we studied the chapter, the unmanned Mariner spacecraft to Mars radioed back high-quality photographs of the Martian surface. Instead of level plains and shallow valleys, the planet turned out to have towering volcano cones, deep meteor craters, spectacular canyons that appeared to be the work of dried up rivers, and vast mountain ranges.

A few years before this, at a different university, I participated in a graduate chemistry course in which the professor explained the procedure for producing xenon difloride. But just less than a decade ago he had required his students to memorize the "fact" that xenon, a member of the inert gases, *could not* form chemical compounds.

How often does this occur? How many scientific "facts" have proven false? This seemed an interesting field of investigation. A short survey revealed an astonishing number of such cases.

Some scientists have the bad habit of thinking

that science—especially the science they learned as students—has all the answers. There is the case of Rudolf Virchow, who flatly refused to believe Pasteur's germ theory as the cause of disease. As time passed other scientists agreed with Pasteur. But Virchow, who had worked in medical research all of his life, simply couldn't come around. He dropped out of medicine and ran for political office in Berlin.

In 1959, Fred Hoyle, the English astronomer, said, "There are no new fields to be opened by the telescopes of the future." Yet, since then dozens of new discoveries have been made—pulsars, quasi-stellar radio sources, black holes, and neutron stars.

Another reason for errors creeping into science is because science is really quite young. Modern science had its beginning in the 1600s. Natural philosophers, as scientists were called then, found discoveries that seemed to disagree with the Bible. Oliver Cromwell, the ruler of England, said to them, "Think it possible science may be mistaken!" But his cry went unheeded.

Because science was young, natural philosophers confidently expected their knowledge to be completely accurate. They did not understand that scientists stumble along at the edge of the unknown. Scientists work by trial and error. Inaccurate information is mixed in with true discoveries, and time is required to separate them.

Today, most scientists are aware of this. They know that the next generation of scientists will put their discoveries to the test and find mistakes.

The Bible has been tested in this way for four thousand years. Is there a science book that will be completely accurate four thousand years from now?

Some people think that science and the Bible cannot agree with each other. This is not the case, as several chapters in this book will show. Max Born, the German physicist who won the Nobel Prize in 1954, said, "Those who say that the study of science makes a man an atheist must be rather silly people."

Science and the Bible are two different ways of looking at the world. One is mainly concerned with spiritual matters; the other with physical matters. But upon occasion the two overlap. When they do, there is no conflict.

One of the greatest scientists of all time, Isaac Newton, spent his younger years studying science. As he grew older he turned to the Bible. He regretted the demand science took upon his time. "It keeps me from the study of Scripture," he said.

When a person states, "Science makes mistakes," he must be prepared to back up that statement with specific examples. That's the purpose of this book.

The cases are not dry recitations of historical events. Instead, this is a moving account of people who were willing to put their reputations on the line by standing up to scientific opinion. Professional scientists have suffered financial disaster because of their unpopular stand. Amateurs have been dismissed as crackpots. Ordinary people have gone through the indignity of trying to express their ideas in the language of science, only to be called superstitious and unlearned.

Hopefully, the reader will find the stories exciting and interesting. This dramatic presentation will not detract from the accuracy of the accounts, but it will make the cases more interesting to read and more easily remembered.

Read on!

1

Pitfalls of Science

Science is something new! Nine out of every ten scientists who ever lived are alive today. At one time the United States had only one scientist of importance. His name was Ben Franklin, and he had to make extra money publishing a little book called *Poor Richard's Almanac*.

Scientists are a cautious group because even celebrated scientists have made embarrassing mistakes. Dr. Vannevar Bush who developed computers was asked if rockets might travel three thousand miles. He said, "I feel confident that it will not be done for a very long period of time." Twenty years later rockets blasted off to the moon!

Have you ever had a lesson at school that makes it seem that science and the Bible disagree with each other? Every Christian has had this happen to him. And when we are young and hear about this for the first time, it causes special trouble.

But the entire universe was set in order by God. The Bible is an accurate description of the universe. Science will not contradict the Bible. Science has no quarrel with religion. True science is simply a way of gaining information about the physical world—but science is not the only way to gain this information.

Because of its newness, science still contains unanswered questions and undisclosed errors which have not yet been weeded out. Scientists who know their business are careful to qualify their conclusions with "as far as I know" or "at this time it seems" and so on.

The Bible, on the other hand, has been put to the test of careful study for more than four thousand years. It has proven itself over the years. Christians should not be too quick to accept scientific "facts" when the "facts" come in conflict with the Bible.

One of the pitfalls between science and the Bible is caused by the fact that the Bible was written before the beginning of science. When the Bible talks about science, the words are not scientific words. Instead, the Bible uses common, everyday language.

As an example of this, a scientist would say that rain is caused by condensation of moisture from the aqueous vapor in the atmosphere. Gravity causes the liquid drops in the atmosphere to fall to the earth.

The Bible, on the other hand, describes rain in this way: "All the rivers run into the sea; yet the sea is not full; unto the place from whence the rivers come, thither they return again" (Eccles. 1:7).

The Bible description is good science. That is exactly how it happens. No matter how the language is changed to put the statement into scientific terms, the Bible account is one of the briefest, most concise, and accurate descriptions of the water cycle. No scientist could improve on it in as few words.

Another pitfall occurs because some words have many meanings. Take *earth* for example. This word may mean something solid, or it could mean the planet on which we live, or ground that is useful for growing crops.

This happens quite often. These changes in the meanings of words make it possible for some people to misunderstand the Bible. Unfortunately, some people want to find difficulties.

The most disturbing reason for differences between science and the Bible is due to some scientists (but not all, by any means) who seem to get a special delight out of attempting to make the Bible appear inaccurate about scientific matters.

Every once in a while these narrow-minded people have taken over science. They welcomed only those who agreed with their point of view. When this happened, the conflict between science and the Bible seemed to be much greater than it actually was.

The Bible was written as a guide for our spiritual life. It is intended to show that man is a sinner and tells him how to be saved. The Bible is not intended to be a textbook about science.

But the Bible is accurate when it does talk about scientific matters. Long ago, the Bible said that the earth hangs upon nothing (Job 26:7). This statement flatly contradicted other views held at that time.

Some of the more ignorant people imagined the earth being carried on the back of a giant turtle. Even the well-educated Greeks imagined that the earth was suspended from a crystalline sphere.

But to us today the idea of earth hanging on nothing doesn't seem strange at all. This idea completely agrees with science. But for thousands of years it seemed the Bible was wrong.

Scientists solve problems by exact methods that usually eliminate errors. Some people read about the "scientific method" and suppose scientists can't make mistakes. This isn't true.

Until recently, astronomers who studied the planets were quite satisfied with their facts about the planet Mercury. This tiny planet is the nearest object to the sun. Mercury couldn't have an atmosphere, scientists reasoned, because the intense heat from the sun would drive off every trace of gas.

Throughout the years William Herschel, who discovered the planet Uranus, and Giovanni Schiaparelli, another skillful observer, had studied Mercury. They made a map of the planet. Apparently Mercury always stayed with the same side facing the sun. Here was a world of extremes, they said, scorched on one side, frozen on the other. Other planets rotate both sides to face the sun. But Mercury would be both the hottest and the coldest spot in the solar system.

This exciting picture of a harsh world baked on one side and frozen on the other isn't true. But scientists must be careful of the human mind, which sees only what it wants to see, not what is actually there. Thousands of observers viewed Mercury through their telescopes and they saw what Herschel and Schiaparelli said they should see.

But recent radar observations with new equipment has proven that Mercury rotates so that both sides of the planet face the sun. All sides of Mercury are equally heated. The temperature isn't as extreme as scientists believed.

To further shake the astronomer's crumbling confidence, radar found that Mercury has an atmosphere! Astronomers accepted the new results in good grace. After all, they had made mistakes before.

During a recent visit to China, an American doctor was surprised to learn that scientists in China invited common people to come into their laboratories to suggest new ideas. Other scientists traveled to farms to work under successful, although uneducated, farmers.

In the United States the idea of a scientist traveling to ask questions of common people seems ridiculous. What could uneducated people know?

How about the Indian rain dance in which silver jewelry is tossed into a fire? Could this cause rain? Is it only a silly superstition?

A rain cloud is made of millions of tiny water droplets too small to fall. However, if the droplets combine to form drops that are large and heavy enough, then the rainfall begins.

Bernard Vonnegut of General Electric Research created a successful rainfall in 1948 by seeding clouds with silver iodide. The small particles of silver iodide provided fine particles that allowed water droplets to collect and form raindrops. Sometimes the trick worked, sometimes it failed.

The Indians, even though they didn't understand the reason, had the right idea. Their fire caused tiny particles of ash and silver to drift up into the clouds. The particles acted as "seeds" around which cloud vapor formed into raindrops. Of course, if there was no water in the sky, then this wouldn't work.

Scientists are just beginning to discover the secrets of God's wonderful world. In the following chapters we'll look at many new exciting and thrilling discoveries.

2

Modern Medicine

Medicine is one of the oldest sciences, but many doctors have refused to accept new ideas. Years ago, some doctors made fun of thermometers for measuring body temperature, others saw no purpose in taking blood pressure or timing the pulse, and others refused to scrub their hands before surgery.

For centuries doctors didn't know how the human body was put together. Anatomy is the scientific name for the study of the body, and the anatomy of the human body is one of the most important things a doctor must know.

The ancient Greeks made the first studies of the human body and its bones. In fact, *anatomy* is a Greek word meaning "to cut." One way to study anatomy is to cut or dissect a body to examine its parts.

Galen, a Greek doctor who lived almost two thousand years ago, dissected animals—dogs, goats, pigs, and monkeys. He described what he saw in careful detail. But not everything he saw in the animals held true in the human body.

For example, he found a network of blood vessels below the brain in most of the animals he investigated, and he considered these blood vessels an important part of the human body. Today we know that the blood vessels Galen described are common in animals, but they are not found in the human body.

Galen was the best doctor who lived during his time. He wrote more than fifty books about medicine, including a sixteen-volume encyclopedia called *On Anatomical Procedure*. His writings were used as textbooks in medical schools for thirteen hundred years.

His books were still being used four hundred years ago when Andreas Vesalius decided to become a doctor. At age seventeen, when he began medical studies in Paris, he was a quick-witted, tough-minded, stocky young man. He would need to be tough-minded to survive what he was about to come up against.

The best-known teacher at the medical school was Franciscus Sylvius. This doctor left surgery to assistants. The messy work of actually touching a patient was too much for his lofty ideas of himself. Instead, Sylvius sat behind a high desk and taught his students by reading from ancient medical books.

The books Sylvius and other doctors read most often were the books of Galen. Although Galen had warned doctors to study firsthand for themselves, his advice had not been taken. Galen had been a successful doctor, and he stated his views with force and confidence. In the centuries that followed him, doctors frowned upon independent study, although that was the only way they could arrive at the true facts about a patient.

Instead, Galen became the undisputed authority. No one dared to differ with his books—books that were thirteen hundred years old.

Franciscus Sylvius, stiff and correct, believed that Galen's books were all a doctor needed to know. Sometimes he did allow a corpse to be dissected under his direction as he read from Galen. But if the corpse and the book didn't agree, then the error was in the corpse!

Andreas Vesalius soon tired of hearing Sylvius read aloud hour after hour from old books. Medicine should be more than a matter of saying "Galen said this," or "Galen said that." He didn't like teachers who taught things they had never tried.

He couldn't bear to watch assistants make hasty, hacking dissections. "I would learn more facts from a butcher in his meat market!" he said.

While still a student, Vesalius resolved that when he became a doctor he would conduct the dissections personally. He wanted to study the human body more accurately.

His chance came when he found a skeleton of a robber that had been left hanging on a gallows. The birds had cleaned the bones. He crept out during the night and cut down the skeleton. This was dangerous business. He could have been thrown into jail.

Back in his room, Vesalius studied the human skeleton until he knew every bone, even while blindfolded.

Sylvius taught that the breastbone had seven segments, yet the breastbone of this skeleton had only three parts. How could his teacher make such a mistake?

Then Vesalius made a horrifying discovery. He compared a monkey skeleton with his human skeleton and found that Galen had studied monkeys instead of humans. Doctors were treating humans with diagrams of monkeys to guide them!

Vesalius found over two hundred mistakes in the ancient books—mistakes still being taught by doctors of his day. He decided to write a new book showing all the muscles and bones.

But he wanted his book to be different. Instead of

long descriptions, he decided to use line drawings that could be easily understood.

He chose Jan Stephen van Calcar, a young artist, to make the drawings. This met immediate opposition by the doctors. What could an artist teach a doctor?

Vesalius's book was published in 1543. The book contained the first accurate illustrations of the human body. The three hundred drawings by Calcar turned out to be not only beautiful works of art, but correct as scientific drawings.

Vesalius's book caused fierce opposition. Other doctors had their reputations at stake. They had taught Galen too long. Every small error of Vesalius's book was pounced upon and hotly scorned.

Sylvius accused Vesalius of all sorts of crimes. For a time Vesalius feared he might be executed. He had to flee Paris.

He wandered from place to place. At age fifty Vesalius traveled to the Holy Land. He visited Jerusalem, and on the way back he died in a shipwreck.

Twenty-five years after the death of Vesalius, William Harvey of England traveled to Padua to study medicine. This was Europe's most famous school, the one Vesalius had attended.

William Harvey was a small man. He had a round face, olive complexion, bright eyes that seldom missed anything, and hair always in need of grooming.

Although Vesalius had proven Galen incorrect about the construction of the human body, the doctors of Padua still accepted Galen's ideas about other matters. They still used Galen's medical books to look up the "right" answer to any problem they had.

The doctors believed veins carried blood out in all directions *away* from the heart. The flow, according to the doctors and to Galen, was slow and irregular. Slowly the blood disappeared to be replaced by new blood from the liver.

Unfortunately, Galen had known nothing of blood circulation—what he believed was completely false. For example, he believed blood surging through the heart caused it to beat. He had no idea that the heart pumped blood.

One of William Harvey's teachers discovered little one-way valves in veins. Harvey wondered about the valves, like little trap doors, which let blood flow only one way. Galen said blood always flowed away from the heart. Yet these trap-doors were turned the wrong way. Blood would flow toward the heart. Something was wrong!

Harvey returned to England and began a successful medical practice. He even had King James I as a patient.

But he still studied the heart. In one experiment he tied closed a vein. Blood caused the vein to bulge on one side, but the side nearest the heart drained empty. Veins carried blood to the heart!

Also, the heart pumps seventy gallons of blood an hour. That's much more than the liver could make. Galen was wrong again. Blood had to be reused, it couldn't just fade away.

William Harvey put his knowledge to use to cure a patient suffering from a large tumor. He tied off the arteries supplying blood to the growth. It withered away.

He published his findings in a little seventy-two-page book, printed on thin, cheap paper. In this book he announced that blood leaves the heart in arteries and returns through veins to be used again.

"How does blood flow from arteries to veins?" doctors asked.

Harvey explained, "There must be tiny tubes between them too small to be seen."

He met bitter ridicule. Many doctors refused to repeat his experiments. Some called him "cracked brained" and frightened away his patients.

After the invention of the microscope, doctors found tiny networks as fine as spider webs connecting arteries to veins. The fine tubes are called capillaries.

Today, three men are given credit for helping modern medicine make real progress. Two of them, Vesalius and Harvey, were physicians. The third man wasn't a doctor at all, but a barber. His name is Ambroise Paré, and he is considered the first modern surgeon.

3

I Dressed Him; God Healed Him

Ambroise Paré grew up at a time when doctors considered surgery beneath their dignity. Instead, they let barbers perform operations as well as cut hair. Surgery wasn't considered a part of medicine.

Ambroise Paré was born of a poor family in the rustic town of Laval, France. He had no formal schooling, and he never learned Latin and Greek, the two languages most needed to study science and medicine.

As a young man he began work as a barber's assistant. The barber shop was the town's first-aid station. The barbers performed minor operations, pulled teeth, and closed cuts. As the barbers gained experience in first aid, they became known as barber-surgeons.

Even today barber poles are striped with red —for blood, and with white—for bandages.

Paré decided to go to Paris to study to become a doctor. But none of the formal medical schools would have him. All of the medical schools in Paris turned him away because he had had only a few years of schooling.

Because the medical books were written in Latin, which the young barber couldn't read, everything he learned came to him by firsthand experience. This turned out just as well. Paré discovered that many of the "facts" in the medical books were inaccurate.

Later, he would say, "Mere knowledge without experience does not give the surgeon self-confidence." He gained more experience as a surgeon than anyone else in Paris, but he still couldn't pass any of the medical examinations —they were in Latin, too.

Instead of attending medical school, Paré found work as a barber-surgeon at the Hotel-Dieu. This "hotel" was actually a hospital for old people and those too poor to care for themselves. The Hotel-Dieu was the first hospital in the world.

Beginning medical students came to the hospital, but they mocked Ambroise Paré because of his poorer education. Most well-to-do patients remained at home and let doctors attend them there. The poor patients at Hotel-Dieu knew Paré as a kind and gentle man with a humble manner so unlike the haughty doctors who sometimes came around to examine them.

In 1536 France went to war, and Paré worked on the battlefields. He went into the thick of the fighting, treating wounds while enemy bullets still fell.

Doctors of Paré's day taught that powder marks from gunshot wounds were poisonous. Their treatment: pour boiling oil into the wound! This horrible treatment was terribly painful, and the boiling oil usually made the wound worse instead of better.

Paré followed this rule until he ran out of oil during a fearful battle. He had to treat the wounds somehow. He made an ointment of eggs, oil of roses, and turpentine. He rubbed the ointment into the wounds.

He expected many of the young soldiers to die, and he hardly slept during the night. The next morning when he made his rounds, he found that the patients with soothing ointment on the gunshot wounds rested far more comfortably than those who were burned by boiling oil.

From then on he used soothing ointment. "I resolved within myself never so cruelly to burn poor wounded men," he said.

Ambroise Paré really cared about his patients. He brought them flowers and cooked them special foods. Once he made a machine to cause the sounds of falling rain to help a patient fall asleep.

This was before pain killers, and there was still much pain even after he stopped using boiling oil to treat wounds. Paré's most horrible duty came whenever a bullet shattered a soldier's leg. Paré had to amputate—cut off—the leg.

After the amputation the stump of the leg had to be seared with a hot iron to close the blood vessels. Otherwise, the victim would bleed to death.

Many young soldiers endured the amputation, including sawing through the bone while fully awake, only to die of pain when the red hot iron was put to their legs.

Unlike the gunshot wounds, soothing oil did no good. The blood vessels had to be closed or the patient would bleed to death. Yet, wasn't there a less painful way? All the great doctors said, "No."

The agony on the faces of Paré's patients became too much. Then Paré hit upon a simple, almost completely painless way to stop the bleeding.

He put a spool of silk thread in his medical kit. At the next amputation he waved aside the hot iron. Quickly he tied the blood vessels closed with thread. Bleeding stopped. As simple as that! His patient lived.

Ambroise Paré, humble as ever, said, "I dressed him. God healed him."

Dr. Gourmelen, one of France's best-known doctors, didn't like this young barber's new success. Dr. Gourmelen said, "To tie the blood vessels after amputation is a new remedy—therefore it should not be used."

The soldiers didn't care about the learned doctor. They loved this young barber-surgeon who spared them from pain. They filled a helmet with silver and gold coins to reward him.

Although Ambroise Paré began as a backwoods barber, he had become France's most skilled surgeon. He always held out hope for a patient. "God often brings things to pass that seem impossible to the surgeon."

After the war ended Paré decided to write about his discoveries. He couldn't write in Latin. Very well, he would write in French. That way other barber-surgeons who couldn't read Latin would be able to read his books.

Dr. Gourmelen didn't like Paré's fame. He tried to block the book. He even charged Paré of stealing his ideas from other doctors. Unfortunately, medical books were printed in Paris, and the law required that all medical books had to be approved by a special group of doctors.

Dr. Gourmelen was on the panel that passed upon new books, and he used his position to enforce the old ways, and conceal his own ignorance. He pretended that he and the other doctors already knew all the answers. Paré was only a barber—not a doctor.

But Paré succeeded in getting his book published. It was an immediate success. During the next few years it went into four editions.

The common people of France made Paré their hero. He became surgeon of King Henry II and to three other kings of France, but he never lost touch with the common people.

He translated Vesalius's book into French so that

barber-surgeons would have a guide to the human body as they made amputations.

Later, he wrote many other books which were noted for their valuable ideas and the ease with which they could be read. He never tried to use big words to sound more profound.

Today the humble barber-surgeon is ranked as one of the greatest surgeons of all time. The people collected enough money to raise a statue of him in France. Under this statue is written: "I dressed him; God healed him."

4

The Pulse and the Pendulum

Archimedes, one of the greatest scientists and mathematicians of ancient times, apologized for his development of the lever and other simple inventions. He thought working with his hands was in poor taste.

At that time, only upper-class people had enough leisure time and money for scientific study and reflection. But because of their position, they considered it disgraceful to build things like common workmen. Very few of the well-to-do performed experiments. Until this attitude changed, research in science couldn't get off the ground.

During the reawaking of learning in the middle of the 1500s in Europe, a new breed of scientists arose who were willing to test their ideas with experimentation. Foremost among them was Galileo Galilei.

Galileo made his first important discovery at age eighteen while a medical student at the University of Pisa. The students attended chapel service each day. One morning in 1581 Galileo noticed a hanging lamp swinging back and forth. The lamp seemed to take no longer to make a big swing then to make a short one.

He returned to his room to try other pendulums. He timed the pendulum with his pulse and found that adding weight to the pendulum didn't change the period taken for a swing. Even pulling the pendulum farther to one side made no difference. The time period remained the same.

Only by lengthening the string could he

lengthen the time for one swing. This simple experiment led to the invention of an accurate clock. And ten years later Galileo developed the first crude thermometer.

Some of Galileo's experiments with falling objects from the Leaning Tower of Pisa made him unpopular with the other professors. He had an uncanny ability to show how utterly wrong they were. He moved to a new position at Padua —where he fared even worse.

The latest hassle came about because of his use of a magnifying tube, or telescope, to study the heavens. When Galileo heard of the instrument which had been invented in Holland in 1609, he immediately saw how important it would be for viewing the night sky.

Aristotle, one of the ancient writers so fondly studied by the men of Galileo's time at Padua, believed the heavens were perfect, without blemish. According to Aristotle the moon was a perfect ball, smooth and polished.

Galileo made a small telescope and turned it to the moon. He discovered mountain ranges, craters, gray plains, and deep valleys. The moon was as rough and uneven as the earth itself. The ancient writings were wrong again!

This discovery made Galileo unpopular. Some scientists even refused to look through his telescope. It threatened their positions. They banded together and forced Galileo to stop publishing his books for many years.

Students, however, enjoyed Galileo's lectures. They filled his lecture halls with standing room only. Teachers who taught by reading from ancient manuscripts found empty seats!

One of Galileo's students was Sanctorius who

was studying to become a doctor. He became convinced that precise instruments such as those invented by Galileo would help doctors treat patients.

Sanctorius recognized temperature as a common signal of a patient's condition during a fever. But how could he measure it? Put his hand on the patient's forehead? No, on a cold day the patient's forehead would feel warmer than it actually was because the doctor's hands would be cold.

The thermometer invented by Galileo couldn't be used to measure body temperature. It was too bulky. But Sanctorius took Galileo's thermometer and perfected it. One of his designs is still in use today.

The pulse rate was another important body sign which Sanctorius wanted to measure. This was before the invention of a reliable clock. But Sanctorius heard of Galileo's experiments with a pendulum and this set his mind to working.

He soon developed a pulse pendulum. He felt a patient's pulse with one hand and let a pendulum swing in his other hand. By changing the length of the pendulum string, he matched the pendulum with the pulse. By marking this point on the string he could return at a later time and check the patient for a change in pulse rate.

He believed that successful treatment would lower the pulse rate, bring the temperature back to normal, and help the patient regain lost weight. Sanctorius also invented an accurate scale to weigh patients.

Not much is known about Sanctorius—the color of his eyes, the way he combed his hair, the friends he visited on Saturday night—but he must have been a careful man who was completely dedicated to putting medicine on a scientific footing. He kept complete records for thirty years to prove the importance of the thermometer and pulse pendulum.

Sanctorius published his methods of measuring the pulse and temperature in 1625. But a hundred years passed before accurate timing of the pulse became common practice. Measuring temperature lagged even farther behind. Two hundred and fifty years passed before a public clinic in Leipzig, Germany, became the first hospital to plot a temperature curve for patients.

Today, in modern hospitals, temperature and pulse rate are the first readings a nurse takes of a patient. Yet, at first doctors considered temperature and pulse rates useless bits of information. The thermometer and pulse pendulum (and later, clock) were only interesting toys without any real application.

Galileo and Sanctorius were well-educated scientists who worked at great universities. History tells of another invention—the microscope—invented and developed by a man who wasn't a professional scientist at all. In fact, he was a simple amateur working with tools found in his home.

Anton van Leeuwenhoek was a Dutchman with very little schooling, who ran a dry goods store and worked as janitor of the town hall at Delft, Holland. These jobs he worked at for the remainder of his life.

But in his spare time he made microscopes. Although it was a hobby, his microscopes were the best in the entire world. He saw things that weren't seen again for a hundred years. Leeuwenhoek made more than 247 microscopes. Some magnified 250 times.

He loved to examine everything with his

homemade microscopes. He looked at fish scales, human hair, and pieces of cork. He wrote about the things he saw and made drawings.

Then one day he noticed tiny moving things not visible to the eyes alone.

He sat back astonished. This couldn't be! All scientists of his time knew that the tiny bug called a cheese-mite was the smallest of all creatures.

But Leeuwenhoek found a fantastic world of little creatures in a drop of water. He wrote up his discovery, not in learned Latin, but in simple Dutch, and sent the letter to the Royal Society of England. The Royal Society was a group of famous scientists.

Most of the members of the Royal Society wouldn't believe his report. They still clung to the story that the cheese-mite was the smallest living thing on earth.

Leeuwenhoek continued to examine many things through his microscope. He looked at canal water, stew broth, even scrapings from his cheek. Everywhere he found little animals—even in drinking water!

Isaac Newton, a member of the Royal Society, suggested a simple way of settling the argument. He directed Robert Hooke, the Royal Society's instrument maker, to construct several microscopes.

Although Hooke's microscopes were not as powerful as those made by Leeuwenhoek, he saw the moving things, too.

The scientists were wrong. The self-educated janitor from Delft, Holland, was right!

At the very limit of his microscope Leeuwenhoek spied tiny moving things, later called bacteria. Robert Hooke's microscopes weren't powerful enough to show them. No one knew or suspected it, but the tiny germs were the cause of disease.

When this fact became known, the microscope became a   permanent tool of medical research.

5

Deadly Doctors

Common sense is what is commonly believed, but this does not make it good sense. If thousands of people believe something for thousands of years, then it must be true! Or must it?

Those tiny microbes wiggling around in Leeuwenhoek's microscope looked too small and harmless to cause disease. It was contrary to common sense.

In 1844, Ignaz Philipp Semmelweis graduated from medical school and immediately accepted a position as assistant director at the Vienna Maternity hospital. During his student days he had become interested in the great killer of young mothers, childbed fever. He decided to track down the cause.

Semmelweis investigated hospital conditions over the objections of Johann Klein who was chief of the hospital. Semmelweis found to his dismay that patients in one ward, where only ignorant midwives worked, seldom had deaths. But in the second ward, where doctors attended the mothers, as many as two hundred fifty of every one thousand patients died. One in four!

The newborn babies fared even worse. One year when thirty thousand babies were born, only five thousand lived long enough to leave the hospital.

Why should a hospital be a place to die instead of a place to live? What caused infection and fever?

"The second ward is nothing more than a murder chamber!" Semmelweis told a friend.

"What causes the fever?"

Semmelweis explained, "It's some type of infection. But the cause is unknown. Johann Klein believes it is induced by overcrowding and poor ventilation."

"And you?" his friend asked.

"I believe the disease is caused by the doctors themselves. They come directly from the dissection room to the maternity ward, carrying infection from mothers already dead with the disease to the healthy mothers they examine."

What could he do to save the lives of these helpless women? He dreaded the ward because of the screams of agony and frightened faces. He patted their hands and tried to reassure them.

The hospital records showed that doctors who wore clean clothes and washed their hands had a better record. More of their patients lived. Could this be the solution?

Semmelweis tested this idea by ordering doctors to wash their hands with soap and water and rinse them in a strong chemical before examining their patients.

He fought a single-handed battle for clean wards and for doctors to wash their hands.

The doctors studied Hippocrates, a Greek physician who had lived two thousand years before. Hippocrates believed diseases could not be carried from one person to the next by contact, and the doctors of Semmelweis's time agreed with him. They resented being told they caused disease.

Yet, the number of fever victims fell way down if they followed Semmelweis's advice. The clinic had a record ten times better than before.

This tremendous success failed to impress Johann Klein the head of the hospital. He was blinded by ignorance and jealousy. He restricted Semmelweis at all steps.

Johann Klein judged the success of a doctor by whether he became wealthy, not by how many lives he saved.

The death rate began to climb again. What could be the cause?

To Semmelweis's horror he found that young doctors were deliberately disobeying his orders! He posted himself out of sight. As he watched, a young doctor who thought he wasn't being observed slipped in to see a patient without dipping his hands in the special chemical solution.

The young doctors enjoyed wearing blood-encrusted examination coats—it made them feel like experienced doctors. They prized the hospital smell about their clothes as a sign of their profession.

Johann Klein agreed with the students. He openly encouraged them. He didn't mind how many patients died, as long as he could keep his pride. He even refused money for Semmelweis to purchase chemicals for the doctors to wash their hands. Finally he prevented Semmelweis's promotion and drove him from Vienna.

Semmelweis never recovered from this blow. He left the hospital troubled by the failure of other doctors to accept his discovery.

True, he didn't understand why cleanliness prevented infection—but he knew it worked. In 1865 he nicked his hand while operating, fell victim to the same disease he had tried to prevent, and died without learning the cause.

Ten years later a young surgeon in Scotland battled a similar problem. Joseph Lister was a surgeon at the Edinburgh, Scotland, hospital. He performed many successful operations. Then he was horrified to see his patients die afterward of infection.

Patients who remained at home for surgery usually survived. But many patients who came to the hospital for even minor surgery died of infection after the operation. No one understood what caused the deadly infection to fill the hospital. Old hospitals became so full of infection they had to be abandoned and burned.

One man came to Lister to have a mole removed from his face as a favor for his bride. The operation was simple and successful. Three days later, however, infection set in and the man died.

Joseph Lister read Semmelweis's paper. He immediately saw the importance of this work. He also read that some scientists had begun to suspect that the tiny microscopic forms found by Leeuwenhoek might be responsible for disease.

If so, then killing the germs would destroy infection. He looked around him and saw doctors examining patients without washing their hands. Before performing operations they donned their "operating coat," one that had been hanging in the operating room for months, used time after time.

Lister knew that germs were everywhere. Germs floated in the air, on the walls of the hospitals and especially on the operating instruments and on the hands of attendants and nurses—everywhere!

Other doctors asked, "Do you say the air is full of these vicious agents? It's too horrible a thought!"

Lister soaked surgery instruments, the operating table, his hands, and the patient with carbolic acid. This killed all germs in the operating room.

The results astonished him. Surgery, usually very risky, became routine.

But his results did not impress the medical world. They called it medical folly. He moved to King's College Hospital in London at age fifty and had to begin all over again. The London doctors openly resented his successful surgery. For a time they organized a boycott and refused to send nurses to help him in the operating room.

But Joseph Lister had a gentle nature, an even temperament, and a resolute will. He tolerated the hostile criticism and let his results speak for themselves.

His methods led to success after success. Doctors could not deny that Lister was right. Hospitals became sparklingly clean places. Lister was the first doctor to be elected to the British Parliament, and scientists elected him president of the Royal Society.

Lister was the ideal physician: skilled, patient, cool, and unselfish. He became physician to the Queen of England. But Lister gave credit where it was due. He said, "Without Semmelweis my achievement would be nothing."

The Old Testament in Leviticus sets forth strict rules concerning contact with corpses, graves, and people with disease. One of the major rules required sick people to avoid contact with other people. After the disease passed, the victim washed carefully and presented himself to the priest. The priest certified him as clean.

For a long time this seemed a strange idea to most people, even to doctors. How could cleanliness cure disease? It wasn't until less than a hundred years ago, following Semmelweis and Lister, that physicians recognized that diseases were caused by germs which could be spread from one person to another by contact.

The old Biblical commands about cleanliness are only another way of showing the truths contained in the Bible. The Bible contains modern scientific discoveries. But the old Biblical commands were in conflict with science and medicine for at least three thousand years.

The Bible tells of Daniel who became a leader because he was ". . . skillful in all wisdom, and cunning in knowledge, and understanding science. . . ." Daniel understood science, but he put faith in God first!

6

Shots That Save

Edward Jenner was a doctor for the village of Berkeley, England. At that time, in 1775, smallpox was a common disease and a dreadful one. When a bad epidemic broke out, as many as one in four people died. Those who did survive weren't completely untouched. The disease caused miserable sores that left awful pockmarks.

But they were lucky in another way. They would never catch the disease again. For some reason, people once exposed to smallpox were safe from being struck again.

For that reason, people intentionally exposed their children to mild cases of smallpox in hopes the children would come down with a mild case, too. It was risky business. Healthy children usually lived. Children in poor health died.

A country girl, who worked on a farm as a milk-maid, told Jenner she didn't need to worry about smallpox. She had caught cowpox, a mild disease which was harmless. But it protected her from smallpox.

Common country people believed this, but doctors called it a silly superstition. Edward Jenner took the story to Dr. Daniel Ludlow. Dr. Ludlow, who had instructed Jenner in medicine, said, "There is no truth in the girl's story."

But Jenner didn't forget the girl's story. As the years passed, he checked out every reported case of smallpox or cowpox around the village.

At first his research puzzled him. Some people

with cowpox later caught smallpox. Could the girl be mistaken?

No, not completely. He did find milkmaids who could care for smallpox victims without fear for their own safety. They never caught smallpox.

Why? Many years passed before Jenner understood the reason. He found the secret when he discovered more than one type of cowpox. Only a certain type of cowpox at a certain time during its development protected from smallpox.

About this time Mrs. John Phipps, one of the local mothers, came to Jenner and pleaded for him to protect her boy. Little Jamie was often sick. He had been so sickly as an infant that she hadn't followed the usual practice of letting him contract a mild case of smallpox. Now she feared Jamie would not be strong enough to survive the next outbreak of smallpox.

Dr. Edward Jenner had been waiting for such an opportunity. He scratched the boy's arm and rubbed fluid from a cowpox blister into the scratch. The boy came down with harmless cowpox.

Two months later the terrible test came. Jenner inoculated the boy again, this time with deadly smallpox. If he failed, the people would call him a murderer—and, indeed, he would deserve that name. But twenty years of study and tests had satisfied him of the result.

Jamie didn't die. He didn't even become sick!

When the village people found out, they called him a cow doctor. One night someone threw rocks through his windows. But they saw Jamie running about and playing like a normal child.

Within a few months other people came to his door and asked to be protected from smallpox. He used a hollowed out goose quill to carry cowpox serum around with him, and with it he inoculated many of the local people.

In 1796, he packed his papers about smallpox and took several goose quills of the serum to London.

At the London Smallpox Hospital the head doctor said, "I'm the world's authority on smallpox, and I know there is no way to prevent smallpox!"

Jenner visited other hospitals. Everywhere he heard the same thing. "Nonsense," the doctors said. "You'll cause children to look like cows." The Royal Society advised him to not tell about his findings—it might ruin his reputation.

After two desperate years, Jenner paid to have a book published telling of his smallpox inoculation.

Normally, such a self-published book would be ignored. But people feared smallpox enough to give his procedure a try. Within eighteen months twelve thousand people in London alone were vaccinated.

He gave up his medical practice to help publicize vaccination. The members of the royal family were vaccinated. Parliament voted him a huge reward. In parts of the world his birthday became a national holiday.

However, English doctors didn't hasten to honor Jenner. At first they laughed at him, and in the end they refused to elect him to the College of Physicians. The College wanted to test his knowledge of Hippocrates and Galen. Jenner decided it was time to oppose the study of such old, out-of-date, doctors. He refused to take the test. In turn, the College of Physicians refused to elect him to the College.

Jenner didn't mind. Vaccination caused smallpox to become a rare disease. Many years passed before another disease was conquered.

Although people in all lands accepted Jenner's

inoculation, or "shots," against smallpox, doctors had no idea of why it worked. They failed to search for shots to protect against other great killers such as cholera, rabies, sleeping sickness, and yellow fever.

After Jenner, a half century passed before the next breakthrough.

Louis Pasteur considered himself a chemist. He won notice with his research into the formation of crystals.

In 1854 he turned to the study of germs. Germs, or bacteria, had been described by Leeuwenhoek. Leeuwenhoek noticed that whenever meat spoiled or milk soured, the number of bacteria increased tremendously.

Scientists thought bacteria sprang into life where there had not been life before. The microscope showed bacteria everywhere—in the air, in water, in food, on the skin, and even inside the body.

Pasteur wondered if the bacteria might cause meat to spoil. Germs might cause disease in humans, too.

Doctors laughed. "You've got it turned around," they said. "Spoiling meat causes bacteria to spring into life."

Pasteur didn't believe in spontaneous generation. He held that all living things must come from other living things. Even the tiniest creatures of God must come from living things like themselves—they did not suddenly arise from nothing.

To prove this, Pasteur left a stew broth in a bottle with a long neck. An elbow bend in the neck allowed air to reach the food, but bacteria would be trapped. The food didn't spoil.

Pasteur proved that gentle heating of the bacteria killed them. Today, pasteurization of milk is an important process for keeping milk fresh for several days.

Pasteur became more and more involved with medicine. Many doctors didn't like this. Pasteur wasn't a doctor—he was a chemist—and he had no right meddling in the affairs of doctors.

For another thing, he overturned their pet ideas. Doctors believed oxygen caused infection. A doctor explained, "A broken bone will not become infected unless the skin is broken."

Pasteur showed bacteria in the air caused infection. His germ theory of disease answered many questions that didn't have a solution otherwise. It explained the success of Semmelweis and Lister in preventing infection.

Pasteur turned his attention to anthrax, one of the oldest and most disastrous diseases to strike farming communities. When an epidemic of anthrax struck the livestock, the only thing to be done was to kill and bury or burn all of the animals. There was no cure for anthrax.

Pasteur showed that all animals diseased with anthrax always had a certain bacteria in their blood. When he injected the bacteria in other animals, they came down with anthrax, too. He correctly concluded that this particular bacteria was the cause of anthrax.

Unlike cowpox, there was not a weak form of anthrax. Very well, Pasteur decided, he would make a weak form.

And he did! The success came when he heated deadly anthrax bacteria. This weakened the bacteria. When he injected them into cattle, they protected the cattle from strong forms of anthrax.

Many doctors objected that germs couldn't cause disease because there was no way that germs could spread from a sick animal to a healthy one.

Pasteur showed that anthrax bacteria could survive for long periods of time in the ground. The soil held the germs, waiting for new victims.

He also showed contact wasn't necessary to spread other disease. Bubonic plague, the Black Death, was carried by a louse that infected rats. The tsetse fly carried sleeping sickness, and mosquitoes carried yellow fever.

Pasteur developed protection against rabies. He saved a young boy who had been attacked by a mad dog. Without Pasteur's treatment the boy certainly would have died.

The people of France collected two and a half million francs to build him a modern laboratory. Doctors who had fought him came forth to claim they thought of the germ theory of disease first!

Although Pasteur never went to medical school, he is considered the greatest doctor of all time.

At the beginning of the twentieth century, medical men had been surprised so many times it seemed impossible for more surprises to be waiting. In fact, some doctors believed all major advances in medicine had been made. As usual, they were wrong—but they hardly expected the surprise from the direction it came.

7

Miracle from Bread Mold

American mothers in early frontier days didn't have a doctor nearby to help when a child cut himself. Sometimes deep wounds became red and inflamed. The mothers scraped mold from bread and rubbed the mold into infected cuts. Strangely, the infected sores healed quickly.

This idea wasn't new. For hundreds of years hot cross buns had been baked early in the morning on Good Friday. We've all heard the rhyme:

> One a penny, two a penny,
> Hot cross buns.
> If you have no daughters,
> Give them to your sons:
> But if you have none of these merry
>   little elves,
> Then you may keep all for yourselves.

Most buns were eaten hot, crossed on top with icing and powdered with sugar. But they put aside two or three buns to be used as medicine for stomach upset.

Doctors scoffed at the idea, and made fun of the backwoods women and their homemade remedies. What could bread mold do? Few believed common substances contained anything of medicinal value.

This wasn't true. Digitalis, an extract from the leaves of the plant called purple foxglove, had been used for centuries to treat heart disease. Quinine was used to repress the effects of malaria. Quinine came from the bark of the quinaquina tree found in South America.

Fifty years ago, in 1925, the mothers and their superstitious notions had been forgotten. Alexander Fleming was a medical student at St. Mary's hospital in London. He checked the patients in his ward and hurried to his laboratory.

In his laboratory he had several small, flat dishes called "petri dishes" in which staphylococcus germs were growing in a jellylike substance. The dishes contained food which the bacteria needed to multiply.

Fleming had put the dishes aside several days previously. Now they needed to be cleaned.

Suddenly Fleming peered closer at a dish. Something had fallen into it and had begun growing in the jellylike material. Around each speck of the new substance, there was a clear ring where the deadly staphylococcus bacteria had been killed and dissolved.

Immediately Fleming saw that the new substance would be useful if it could kill disease bacteria. Of course, the new substance might also kill the cells of animal life as well. All the germ killers then in common use were more dangerous to human cells than they were to bacteria. To be really useful, his discovery would have to destroy germs without killing human cells.

Fleming transferred a part of the substance into new petri dishes, and there it grew until there was enough to inject into mice. The mice were not harmed. Here was something special.

Fleming named the new substance—a type of bread mold—penicillin.

Penicillium mold is a tiny, simple plant which belongs to the fungi group. It is related to mildews, rusts, and mushrooms.

Molds develop from spores. When a spore settles on damp food substances such as bread, it swells and begins to grow by putting out tiny threads.

44

Apparently, the mold also produced a chemical which was a powerful germ killer.

If penicillin could be made in large amounts, it would be very useful to stop infections. But to make it, Fleming needed assistants trained in chemistry and a better laboratory. So he reported the discovery and hoped that someone with a better laboratory would make the life-saving chemical.

For fifteen years, Fleming's discovery went unnoticed. But when World War II began, it became important to have a substance which would stop infections. More people were dying from disease and infection than from bullets and bombs.

Howard Florey, another English scientist, studied the bread mold. He found that it was even more powerful than Fleming had thought. When Florey diluted the yellow-brown chemical a million parts to one, it still killed germs. But it was very difficult to extract the chemical.

After several months, Florey had eight hundred milligrams of penicillin. This is less than one twenty-fifth of an ounce!

In a nearby hospital, the doctors were trying to save the life of a policeman who had blood poisoning. The policeman's temperature climbed to 105 degrees, and the doctors did not think he would live for another day. They heard of the amazing new chemical and asked Florey to try to save their patient.

Florey diluted the drug so he could stretch it over several doses. After the first injection, the policeman's temperature dropped, his breathing became easier, and his face, which had been red and puffed, began to look normal.

The next day the temperature went up again, so

Florey gave the man another dose of penicillin. Again, there was improvement.

By the fourth day the doctors could see that the patient would recover. Then, horrified, they learned that Florey had run out of penicillin! It would take him weeks to make more. The doctors watched helplessly as the patient's temperature rose. Finally, he died.

Florey resolved to learn better and faster ways to make penicillin. But England was being bombed each night by the German Air Force. The factories that had not been destroyed by bombs were needed to produce other goods.

Florey and the English scientists and doctors decided to ask the United States to help. They came to America and gave the secret to a dozen drug manufacturers.

The American scientists quickly discovered that penicillium mold could be grown within the jelly-like substance, as well as upon its surface. They built huge vats with paddles to stir the mixture as the mold grew all through it.

Until then the total amount of penicillin that had been made was only two ounces. During 1945, more than six tons were produced.

Today the miracle chemical produced by bread mold is the best weapon doctors have to fight infection.

Both Florey and Fleming were knighted by the queen, and in 1945 they shared the Nobel Prize in medicine for their work with penicillin.

Old folk remedies are making good. Ancient books are being read a second time in hopes of finding clues to new sources of drugs.

Explorers search the world, looking for new and unusual plants that might contain a valuable extract that cures disease. In Saint Louis, Missouri, the botanical gardens has a special vault which contains more than three million different types of plants.

Half of all drugs come from plants and herbs. Plants produce thousands of medical substances that can be used directly, or chemists can use them as models to produce drugs synthetically.

The creation of God is so bountiful that many surprising secrets still remain to be revealed. Scientists cannot help but marvel at the healing agents which God provides in nature.

8

The Strange Case of the Uncooperative Pea Plants

Gregor Johann Mendel rubbed his fingers across the wrinkled leaf of the pea plant. He shook his head, puzzled. Something was wrong. Few of the experiments with pea plants in the tiny garden behind the school in Troppan, Austria, were going as scientists predicted they should.

Mendel was not a famous scientist. He had survived a miserable childhood of poverty and hardships. He couldn't go to school regularly, so he was largely self-taught.

But his knowledge of science earned him a place as an elementary school teacher. To keep the job he had to go back to school. He took a teacher's examination, but failed. On a second try several years later, he failed again.

He became a teacher anyway, and took to teaching with pleasure, although he had to teach all of his life with a temporary teacher's certificate. His upright life led him to become a priest in 1847.

He and his students got along with good humor. He collected a roomful of wild creatures such as a fox, hedgehog, mice, and a cage of birds.

He wanted to study heredity, how certain characteristics are transferred from parent to offspring. He couldn't bear the thought of using mice in experiments, so he decided to use pea plants. The school was poor, so he had to choose simple, inexpensive equipment. It couldn't be much simpler than this—a plot of ground and a bag of peas!

Mendel grew a variety of tall pea plants, and a variety of dwarf pea plants. When he cross-pollinated the two types, the result should be a plant of average size. At least that's what should have happened according to Francis Galton, the well-known English scientist. Galton and several other students of heredity said that plants should be a balanced blend of parent plants.

But most of Mendel's plants grew tall, some grew dwarf. None were in-between!

Mendel searched for a mistake in his procedure. He couldn't believe that Francis Galton was in error. This great scientist had come from a family that provided him with a splendid education at King's College and Trinity College, Cambridge, England. Galton could speak five languages. After graduation he had traveled around the world, wrote many books and became a member of the Royal Society. He made important discoveries in many fields, and in 1906 the queen knighted him.

Could Galton be mistaken? Mendel tested again by crossing wrinkled-leaved pea plants with smooth-leaved pea plants. The result should have been a plant with slightly wrinkled leaves. Again, the results surprised him. This time all the leaves were wrinkled. None were smooth!

Of course, other people tackled the mysteries of heredity, too. It was an important problem. Farmers and ranchers would be able to grow better crops and raise better livestock if they could predict what caused changes from one generation to the next.

Other scientists in well-equipped laboratories all over the world engaged this problem. However, most of them chose more ambitious subjects to study. They experimented with mice, monkeys, and even humans.

Francis Galton in England had tried his hand at heredity. He decided upon an impressive study of three thousand English families. This study, he said, would give a simple law to explain why some children look like their parents and others do not.

He sifted through tons of data, studied hundreds of twins and more than nine thousand individuals. But years of study resulted in only minor discoveries in this field, although he did win fame in other areas.

One scientist summed up Galton's research by saying, "Galton concluded that, in general, parents with big feet tend to have children with big feet!"

While Francis Galton did this, Johann Mendel continued with his pea plants. Finally, after sixteen years of watching them grow in the garden, he caught onto the secret.

When he kept the tall plants on one side of the garden, and the dwarf plants on the other side, the tall plants always produced seeds which grew into tall plants.

These plants which always bred true he called *purebred*.

Slowly, by using mathematics, Mendel figured out the mystery. He developed the idea of dominant and recessive genes. Some characteristics will dominate over other characteristics. Tall pea plants are dominant. Dwarf is recessive.

Mendel worked for months getting his report ready to present to scientific publications.

When Gregor Johann Mendel's paper arrived they could only smile in disbelief. The scientists who screened papers for publication knew Galton had failed, and was an unknown grade school teacher trying to tell them he had found the secret of heredity by studying peas? His theory completely contradicted the commonly accepted notions. A priest who mixed biology and mathematics. They returned the paper. Sorry.

Mendel tried again and again. Each time they returned his paper.

In 1864, the local scientific society met. This small group was a hodgepodge of doctors, teachers, chemists, biologists, and astronomers. They listened to his report about the pea plants. But they couldn't understand what Mendel was doing. Who had ever heard of combining biology with mathematics?

Mendel's work would have been completely lost, except for the fact that the local society printed the lectures given before it. They printed Mendel's lecture and sent it to several universities around Europe.

Mendel sent a copy of this report to Karl von Nägeli, a Swiss botanist. Unfortunately, Karl von Nägeli was old-fashioned, bad tempered, and in poor health. He believed ideas were more important than experiments.

Nägeli read Mendel's report. He sent it back with a letter which clearly implied that Mendel had a nice little experiment which was very interesting but not very important. He dismissed the report in polite terms.

It was the same old story. Mendel knew his methods worked, but he hadn't developed a scientific-sounding theory to explain why they worked.

Mendel died at the monastery in 1884. He was buried as a simple monk. Those who mourned for him didn't know that he would one day be recognized as the founder of modern heredity.

For many years his little paper in the local

society's journal gathered dust. Then in 1900, H. De Vries in Holland discovered the little journal in a stack of dusty magazines in the corner of a library in Amsterdam. For thirty-five years it had been overlooked. But De Vries instantly saw that Mendel had succeeded where others had failed.

Even Francis Galton recognized the importance of the paper.

Why had Mendel succeeded? Apparently the other scientists had been too ambitious. The animals they studied were too complex. Mendel, in his simple-minded way forced upon him by poverty, had chosen pea plants.

After Mendel became famous, the townspeople of Altbrunn replaced the simple grave marker with a large statue. The inscription says, "To the Investigator of Nature." Today, few people have heard of Francis Galton or Karl von Nägeli, but every biology student learns of dominant and recessive genes first revealed by Gregor Johann Mendel.

9

Fingerprints

Have you ever called to a friend who was a great distance away and then, as he turned, discovered you had called to the wrong person? This is an embarrassing mistake of identification that we all make.

Proper identification has caused problems for a long time. Even in the Bible, Isaac mistook his son Jacob for Esau because Jacob's arm had been dressed in goatskin.

One of the first modern methods of identification of people was developed by Alphonse Bertillon in France. He used body measurements such as the length of the skull, the length of each foot, the size of the ears, and peculiar markings such as scars.

These measurements, as well as photographs, were quickly taken up by police throughout the world. But there were problems. The method was useful only for people between the ages of twenty and sixty-four because the sizes of bones change as children grow, and they shorten when people pass the age of sixty-four. The measuring had to be done carefully. The Bertillon method required a skillful person to press the instruments with exactly the same force and arrive at the same measurements each time.

But for centuries there had been another way of identifying people, a method scientists had overlooked. Fingerprints were used a thousand years ago by the Chinese who put inked thumbprints on papers as signatures.

Before the birth of Christ a Babylonian officer recommended taking the fingerprints of robbers.

Fingerprints are patterns left by tiny ridges on our fingers. Doctors call the tiny ridges *friction ridges* because they help us pick up small objects. Without friction ridges smooth coins would slip from our grasp.

In Italy in 1680, Dr. Marcello Malpighi tried to interest fellow scientists in fingerprints. "I look at the end of a finger and perceive these ridges to be drawn out in loops and whorls." But he didn't interest them. (He did, however, discover with a microscope the capillaries that carried blood from arteries to veins. This verified Sir William Harvey's study of blood circulation).

Two hundred years passed. In 1858, James Herschel, the grandson of the British astronomer who discovered the planet Uranus, worked as a government clerk in Bengal, India. His duties included giving checks for pensions and allowances to the Bengalese. But many criminals appeared with forged identification papers and demanded the pensions of other people. These criminals even went so far as to cut identical scars so they would appear as the person they were impersonating.

James Herschel spent weeks in court trying to establish the proper identification of suspected forgers.

That's when he became interested in fingerprints. He required all people to be fingerprinted when they came for the money. This quickly brought to light those who were dishonest.

Herschel reported his success to the head of Bengal's prison, suggesting his fingerprint system might help identify inmates who returned to prison a second time.

Then, as now, judges gave second offenders stiffer sentences because the criminals had repeated their crimes. Of course, most criminals changed their names and avoided the longer sentences. Herschel pointed out that they couldn't change their fingerprints.

But Bertillon's body measurements had become standard practice with the police. Bertillon himself ridiculed and completely rejected the fingerprinting idea. "My system assures positive identification when performed by an expert," Alphonse Bertillon said.

Herschel's use of fingerprints was almost forgotten by the police in Europe. But in 1903 the United States Prison System at Leavenworth Penitentiary in Kansas decided to use both body measurements and fingerprints on a trial basis.

Early one morning a new prisoner was brought before the officer at Leavenworth. "William West," the officer read on his card. He began taking William West's Bertillon measurements. "You've been here before," the officer said. "I remember you."

"You're mistaken," the prisoner said.

"We'll see about that," the officer said. He completed the measurements and checked through the other cards. "Here it is." He held up a card bearing the name of William West, a photograph of the man, and Bertillon measurements.

"That looks like my picture, all right," the prisoner said. "I don't know how you got it. But this is my first time in prison."

Another guard looked over the card. He remembered that Leavenworth did have another prisoner named William West. The prison officer sent for the other man.

"Here he is," the guard announced.

In walked the other prisoner. The guards stared in disbelief. The two prisoners examined each other in amazement. The two men were identical in every way—like looking into a mirror.

The Bertillon system had failed. The two men had body measurements precisely alike, their photographs looked the same, and they even had the same name!

Then the officer took their fingerprints. The patterns were different. Only in this way could he tell the two men apart.

Fingerprints overshadowed the Bertillon system after that. Scientists found that every human carried with him a signature at the end of his fingers. This autograph cannot be changed nor hidden, and it is personal. There are no duplicates among the millions of people on earth.

It is impossible to rub out the fingerprint ridges. Although they are only one twenty-fifth of an inch thick, they grow back in exactly the same pattern.

Palm and feet prints are taken of newborn babies to avoid mix-ups at hospitals.

Yes, we have friction ridges on our feet, too. One crook took off his shoes so he could use his socks to cover his hands as he broke into a house. That way he left no fingerprints—but the police found him out because he left behind feet prints!

Many Biblical scholars believe that the ancient prophets of the Old Testament understood about fingerprints. Job says about God, "He sealeth up the hand of every man that all men may know his work."

Another ancient writer says that men can make millions of coins all alike, but God creates billions of human beings of whom no two are alike.

10

The Bible Today

More than five hundred years ago, before Columbus discovered the New World, books were something special that had to be protected and kept in museums or churches or in the homes of rich people. The Bible was the most important book of all.

No wonder it was so special. It had to be written by hand. This tedious work was done by monks who lived in monasteries. To copy the Bible required a full year of work, and a Bible with fancy patterns and pretty designs took even longer. For that reason, few people had a Bible of their own. These handwritten books were very expensive. The owner of a Bible or a dozen other books could be considered a rich man.

Another method of printing a book was to cut a wooden block exactly like a page but with all the words and drawings reversed, like in a mirror. The printer coated the block with ink and pressed parchment, a type of paper made from animal skin, against the inked block. Hundreds of sheets could be printed from one block.

But carving a block took months. Each page of a book required a new block. To print the entire Bible this way would require a lifetime.

Johann Gutenberg, who was a stonecutter and mirror maker, had the inspiration which made the Bible available to everyone.

He reasoned, "Books are made up of the twenty-six letters of the alphabet and ten symbols such as the period, comma, quotation mark, and so on. Suppose the letters could be reused. The letters could be made separately and put together as a block. A thousand copies of a page could be printed, then the same letters rearranged to form a new page. This could continue until the entire Bible is printed."

It was in 1436 that Gutenberg set out to find a way of making type bars with a single letter at the tip of each one.

He tried wood first. It was a failure. The tiny wooden sticks were difficult to carve, even harder to make exactly the same size, and when they were locked together to make a page, the ink softened the wood and caused blurred, messy pages.

He tried lead next, but it was too soft. The paper pressed against the lead type and caused it to flatten out. He tried iron, but it was too hard.

He worked for years. The money he had saved while a stonecutter and mirror maker slowly disappeared into unsuccessful experiments. The printing press with movable type seemed as far away as when he had first begun. Gutenberg ran out of money.

After a short delay, two friends offered to help. Gutenberg decided to scrap everything and begin all over. This time he did everything himself from scratch. He made his own printing press, he prepared a special ink, he ordered a special type of paper. He found that copper worked for making letters.

In 1456, Gutenberg announced publication of the first book make by movable type. The book was the Holy Bible. Its cost? About four dollars. His dream of a Bible everyone could own and read for themselves had come true.

As soon as inexpensive copies of the Bible became practical, several translations appeared. The Bible, originally written in Hebrew, had been translated into Greek, then Latin, and finally into English and other languages. For the first time common people had a Bible they could read in everyday language.

Critics of the Bible said, "Suppose that during all those years when scribes copied the Bible, they made mistakes. Small errors would become large mistakes as they recopied the Bible year after year."

They pointed to the King James Translation, the most popular and best known of the English translations. The critics believed the manuscripts used to make that translation could not be trusted.

A reply to this criticism came in 1947, not by famous scientists, but by two young boys tending their goats.

The pair of boys, Arab goatherders, tended their goats in a valley called Wadi Qumran, near the Dead Sea. The valley is windswept and barren. Short and scrubby vegetation, barely fit even for goats to eat, fights for a place in the worn-out soil.

The valley walls are almost sheer, broken in places by caves hollowed out by wind and time. Inside the caves wild animals make their homes.

One day a goat strayed from the boys' herd. They searched the valley carefully. Finally they decided the lost animal had to be in one of the caves. They had waited to search the caves until last because of the darkness and danger.

They checked out a cave before entering by tossing in a stone. In one cave they didn't hear the cry of an animal. Instead, they heard the sound of breaking pottery.

They entered the dark, foreboding cave through

a tiny opening that led to a dusty, rough chamber. The goat was not inside. But at one time something had lived inside—people!

Eight tall clay jars stood along the back wall, one of which had been broken by the stone. Inside it was an ancient scroll. Two smaller scrolls were found in the other jars.

The scrolls had been written before the time of Christ. Thirty-eight scrolls were found in all. They contained the text of nineteen books of the Old Testament. They were written on leather and papyrus. The script became known as the Dead Sea Scrolls.

Two thousand years ago, the Essenes, a strict group of Jews, gathered many old Biblical manuscripts together and stored them in the caves. They hid away most of the books of the Old Testament.

Suddenly, with one leap, scholars had Bible manuscripts twice as old as any others they had studied.

The old scrolls could be used to answer the critics' question; "Is the Bible of today the same as the one written by the prophets?"

Scholars made a careful word-by-word comparison of the Dead Sea Scrolls. Learned men who didn't believe the Bible as the Word of God expected a great many differences.

They found no important errors. The accuracy of the Bible is amazing. Of every ten thousand words, scholars can agree upon the spelling and word order for nine thousand nine hundred and ninety-nine. Only one word in ten thousand offers any trouble in trying to figure out. These troublesome spots are caused by difficult names or variations on simple words that cause no real trouble with understanding the meaning of the Bible.

God guided the hands of the men who copied the Bible. Isaiah of the Old Testament says, "The grass withereth, the flower fadeth: but the word of our God shall stand for ever" (40:8).

Other books have been destroyed by fire, or lost, or changed by time. Not the Bible!

11

Digging into the Bible

For a long time critics considered the Bible inaccurate about historical matters, and some went so far as to say that the Bible writers collected little stories which had no basis in fact. "The Bible contradicts true history," they said.

For example, Luke said that when Christ was born, "about this time Caesar Augustus, the Roman Emperor, decreed that a census should be taken throughout the nation. (This census was taken when Quirinius was governor of Syria)" (Luke 2:1-2, The Living Bible).

Every so often Rome took a census and counted Roman citizens as well as all other people ruled by the empire. They did this to collect taxes from the people of conquered lands to support Rome.

For centuries scientists found no evidence of the census Luke described. Yes, there had been other counts of the people, but not at the time Luke mentioned.

Historians found that Quirinius was one of the rulers of Syria. He did carry out a census in A.D. 6 and 7, but that one could not be the one described by Luke, because Jesus would have been a young boy by that time. The Bible was wrong about the census, scholars decided.

But recently an inscription in an old temple in Angoral, Turkey, came to light. The temple had been built by Augustus who was Rome's first emperor. The inscription in Latin described a census which Quirinius had taken, but this one didn't match the one scientists knew about.

Another Roman inscription at Antioch revealed the surprising fact that Quirinius had been the emperor's legate in Syria on a previous occasion. Quirinius had ruled in Syria two separate times! Archaeologists did not know of the first time. They had knowledge only of the second time.

During the first reign, Quirinius had taken a census which perfectly matched the one described by Luke. Luke knew his facts about the trip of Joseph and Mary. The historians who doubted him were proven wrong.

History, science, and the Bible come together with archaeology. Archaeology is the scientific study of the lives and times of people who lived in the past. We usually think of archaeologists as digging up bits of pottery, searching out hidden Egyptian tombs, or finding the ruins of lost cities.

Archaeologists have made many surprising discoveries about the Bible.

Take the Biblical account of the wealth of Solomon. Historians believed his great wealth had been exaggerated. Solomon would have needed enormously rich mines, and none had been discovered in Israel.

Scientists had another objection. The Bible tells of a huge brazen sea and pillars of the temple that were made of copper. They dismissed these stories because King Solomon's workmen didn't have the skill needed to extract copper from ore. Gold and silver would have been easy to melt from rocks, but copper was another matter.

Then in the early 1900s explorers found the mines. They were far away in the rough hill country of Jordan at the edge of the Arabian Desert. Solomon's men worked the mines centuries ago, but they are still rich even today. In fact, some of the mines have been put back into production.

What about the copper? In 1937, scientists solved the mystery. They found a copper smelter. King Solomon's metal workers had made one of the first blast furnaces. The source of compressed air was the wind itself. In the windy hill country they crossed a valley pass with a funnel-shaped stone tunnel. The tunnel caught wind and guided it to the smelter. This was three thousand years ago. It was one of the first uses of a blast of air to make a furnace burn hotter.

The accuracy of the Bible comes from the fact that God guided the men who wrote it. The men were not writing what they thought, but what God had commanded them to write. The statement "Thus saith the Lord," or statements similar to this, are found more than three thousand times in the Old Testament.

But there is outside evidence of the Bible's accuracy. Moses mentions a sevenfold lamp. For a long time critics of the Bible thought this section of the Old Testament had been added at a later date. The sevenfold lamp had not been invented when Moses lived. But at Dothan in 1962, workmen uncovered such a lamp that came from the time of Moses.

Many of the ancient tribes in the Old Testament are not mentioned anywhere else. This upset some historians. The Hittites figure in many of the stories in the Bible. But historians had not uncovered any remains of such a people. Critics pointed to this as an example of the mistakes found in the Bible.

But over the last few years archaeologists have uncovered clay tablets containing Hittite laws and entire cities put up by the Hittites. Ancient records, recently discovered, mention the Hittites. In every case, these new facts have exactly fitted in with what the Bible said about this so-called lost civilization.

One after another the supposed inaccuracies in the Bible have been eliminated. Time after time new discoveries come to light which show that the supposed errors in the Bible were errors of the archaeologists and scientists instead. The scientists didn't have all of the information. The Bible in I Samuel 2:3 says, "For the Lord is a God of knowledge."

12

Nineveh Is Found

Probably the greatest attack upon the Bible began one hundred years ago when people called the Bible a Hebrew myth.

For example, according to the Bible, ancient Nineveh was the capital of Assyria. Nineveh had a population of 120,000 people, and the city was so large a person needed three days to walk across it. Nineveh had been founded by Nimrod, the great-grandson of Noah.

Later, the city became so wicked God sent Jonah to cause the people to repent. He prophesied disaster because of the city's wickedness. The people did repent for a time. Then they became wicked again and turned to false gods. Nahum says, "God will not acquit the wicked. . . . Nineveh is full of lies and robbery" (1:3; 3:1).

God promised to destroy the city this time. In Zephaniah 2:13 the Bible says, "And he will stretch out his hand against the north, and destroy Assyria; and will make Nineveh a desolation, and dry like a wilderness."

Scientists couldn't believe the Biblical story of Nineveh. It couldn't be as large as the Bible said. They pointed out that a city of 120,000 people would need a tremendous supply of water, but Nineveh didn't have modern pumps to supply water.

A city the size of Nineveh simply couldn't disappear! Even today, after three thousand years, something would have to remain. But not a single stone from the city of Nineveh had been found. Either

Nineveh didn't exist, or it wasn't as large as the Bible claimed.

The narrow-minded people who dominated science at that time didn't welcome anyone except those who had studied at well-known universities.

However, Paul Emile Botta, the French trade representative to Iraq, decided to look for ancient Nineveh. Botta was an amateur, and he believed the Bible would be a good guide as he searched for the site of ancient Nineveh.

Paul Emile Botta was stationed in Mosul, Iraq. Iraq is the modern name for the ancient country of Assyria. Mosul was an out-of-the-way city. To reach it Botta had to travel up the Persian Gulf, follow the Tigris River past the old city of Baghdad until he reached Mesopotamia.

At one time Mesopotamia was a rich land that grew good crops. The kings of Syria, Babylonia, and Assyria fought for Mesopotamia. Mesopotamia means "land between the rivers." The rivers are the Tigris and Euphrates. But only the Bible told about the kings. Nothing remained in Botta's time except a desert of black soil and strange hills which rose above the flat deserts.

The mounds had flat tops and steep sides. Most were covered with tough camel-thorn and other dry brush, although some of the mounds were used to grow wheat. All along the deserts of Assyria these strange mounds had stood for centuries. No one knew what had caused them.

Botta first began by hunting for pottery or bricks from the city of Nineveh. His job as a trade representative took him to the noisy market places. Iraq was a poor country and the people were thrifty. It was possible that bricks or pottery from ancient Nineveh might still be used by the people of the day, handed down from generation to generation.

But he had to give this up. The people did have old clay pots, but they didn't know where the pottery had come from.

Botta turned his attention to the mounds. He dug into one of them. He worked for a year. It is difficult to imagine the hardships he faced. He was a stranger among the Arabs, and they didn't trust foreigners. He had to endure the stifling heat, and all he found were a few broken bricks and pieces of cracked statues.

But Botta was young and strong. He brushed away the insects that carried all kinds of disease, he shrugged off the terrible heat, and he outmaneuvered the Arab governor who didn't want him to dig into the mounds.

He moved to two more of the strange mounds on the Tigris River just six miles from his home base of Mosul, Iraq.

The mound wasn't a mountain at all. It was a city! At one time date palms had grown around it, and fields grew wheat and barley. But for some unknown reason the city was abandoned. Thousands of years ago the wind blew sand and covered the city completely. Finally, the mighty ruins were lost in the desert. No trees grew to shade the weary traveler against the burning sun. The land became poor and unproductive. Wandering goatherders stopped to graze their animals and gave no thought to the tremendous mounds.

Botta continued digging. Scientists studied his reports. They were astonished.

The first mound was a summer palace for the Assyrian kings. Beautiful white alabaster covered the walls. Ancient artists had carved pictures into the alabaster showing the daily life of the palace.

Here was the home of Ashurbanipal, Sargon, and Nebuchadnezzar! All of these kings are mentioned in the Bible. Botta cleared away the rubble and found courtyards, public reception rooms, corridors, and even a zoo and place for flower gardens.

Botta's excavation of the second mound of dirt showed the main city of Nineveh.

He found frightening animal figures—winged lions with human heads. The people of Nineveh had turned away from the true God and worshiped strange gods.

He also found an elaborate system of eighteen canals to bring water from the hills north of Nineveh.

He uncovered a library containing dried clay tablets. The tablets contained cuneiform writing which told the history of Nineveh.

The library described Nineveh as the largest city of the ancient world. Its history came to an end when Chaldeans and Medes destroyed the city, as the Bible said.

Today scientists give credit to Botta for finding one of the world's oldest cities. They owe much to this amateur archaeologist who refused to stop digging. He uncovered a lost chapter from the book of history. Because of his success, men have taken up an inquiry into other events contained in the Bible.

13

The Ark on Ararat

An unbeliever questioned how forty days of rain could flood the earth. "There are places on earth where rain falls every day all year around. But the land doesn't flood."

A person who knew the Bible answered this question by pointing out that the Bible says that not only did the windows of heaven open, but also the fountains of the great deep broke up. The earth contains fifty times as much water in the ground as it does in rivers. Here was the source of water that flooded the earth. It had welled up from the ground.

What of Noah's Ark? The Bible tells that it came to rest in the Armenian mountains in Turkey near Russia's border where Mount Ararat is the highest peak.

For a long time scientists discounted the story of Noah and the Ark. But a few years ago the discoveries of Nineveh and King Solomon's mines made them take a closer look at the mountain called Ararat.

Mount Ararat is the highest peak in Turkey, two hundred miles north of Nineveh. It is a towering volcanic peak with sulphurous fumes seeping from rocks along its slopes.

An amateur explorer named Fernand Navarra decided to see what he could find. First, he read the ancient historian Josephus who described a ship in an icy grave on the snow-covered summit of Mount Ararat. Next, Marco Polo, famous early explorer, said, "It is in this very country [Turkey] that the Ark exists—a place where the snow is so constant that no one can ascend where the snow never melts."

At one time a small monastery at the foot of the mountain is said to have contained a very ancient wooden fragment that came from the Ark. But in 1840 an eruption of the volcano on Mount Ararat caused an earthquake and landslide which buried the monastery. The landslide swept away the entire village of Nazuana at the foot of Mount Ararat. In Armenian, Nazuana means "Here Noah settled."

Nearby is another village named Aghur where, according to tradition, Noah built his altar and made sacrifices after his safe deliverance from the Ark, and where he also planted his vineyard.

In modern times a Russian airplane pilot named Roskovitsky flew over Mount Ararat and glimpsed the dark shape of a ship in the glacial ice. He convinced the Russian government of his impressive discovery. The Russian czar sent 150 men on an expedition to the mountain.

Some say they located the Ark. The world will never know for sure. What happened? When the men returned, the Russian revolution overthrew the czar and put in power a communist regime. The new government didn't believe in the Bible. They destroyed all records of the expedition.

Again, in 1952 a helicopter pilot took pictures of a prow sticking out of glacial ice. This was fourteen thousand feet up on the mountain, and three hundred miles from trees large enough to make an ark!

Until Fernand Navarra, no scientists had actually brought back a piece of the wood. So there was only one thing left for Fernand Navarra to do. He would climb the mountain himself! It wasn't an easy job. The Turks call Ararat *Agri Dagh* which means Mountain of Agony.

Navarra spent his own money to outfit an expedition. As they climbed in early spring they underwent incredible difficulties. Swirling snow blinded them and made climbing unbearably cold and dangerous.

Cold changed into sunny weather. This didn't end their hardships. Instead, sunlight melted snow which loosened huge boulders which tumbled down the glacier. The men in the expedition scattered. Navarra had to be extra cautious because a landslide like the one that leveled the village of Nazuana might sweep away his men and equipment.

Near the summit Fernand Navarra made his discovery. Wind had blown snow away. The ice was clear. Deep in an icy grave below his feet Navarra found the dark form of a massive hull. A great boat was frozen in the glacier!

He described his discovery. "We found an astonishing patch of blackness within the ice, its outline sharply defined. The shape was unmistakably that of a ship's hull."

But how could he get to the Ark? The shifting glacier had trapped it deep in the heart of the ice, much too deep to reach by chipping away at the ice.

He solved his problem when he found where hot sulfur steam escaping from the partially extinct volcano had melted a cavern in the floor of the glacier. Navarra explored the cave in the ice and reached a beam of the ship which stuck out, free of ice.

He sawed away a five-foot-long fragment of the beam. Tarlike substance covered the wooden plank, and it had been hand tooled. The Madrid

Institute of Forestry in Spain estimated its age at about five thousand years. The exact age can't be determined accurately. Glacial meltwater had soaked the wood for many centuries, and sulfuric gases and sulfurous acid had damaged the wood fibers.

What else is known about the structure on Mount Ararat? Everyone agrees that it is in the shape of a ship. The timbers are very old, and the wooden ship is in a place where no trees grow. The location, fourteen thousand feet above sea level, is wild and desolate, high above the timber line and far from any people.

Is the structure a temple in the shape of an ark? Is it an ark made as a model of the original Ark? Or is it the Ark that Noah made? Fernand Navarra thinks so. He has written a book called, "I Found Noah's Ark."

The Ark on Ararat is not ignored anymore. Scientists have spent one million dollars to equip an expedition to uncover more of the handmade vessel.

14

Eighteen Hours in a Whale

One of the most exciting Biblical stories is about Jonah and his three days in the belly of a great sea creature. For a long time some people called this story only a dream. Scientists believed that the digestive juices of most whales are so potent that any man swallowed would meet instant death.

But a British sailor named James Bartley proved these ideas incorrect when he was swallowed by a whale—and lived to tell about it!

His astonishing story is told by records of the British Admirality. In 1888, James Bartley had gone to sea in *The Star of the East,* a whaling vessel. At that time whaling ships were floating factories, large and cumbersome, and they couldn't sail very fast.

A lookout on the mast stood watch in the crow's nest to search for whales. Whales are mammals like horses and cows, and they must come to the surface to breath air.

When the whale surfaces, he clears his air hole with a mighty blow. The lookout in the crow's nest can see this spray of water from a great distance.

Early one morning James Bartley heard the lookout in the crow's nest yell, "There she blows!" He and the other sailors ran to the longboats.

Because the whaling ship was so slow, the whales were hunted by smaller and faster longboats manned by sailors pulling oars. This time James Bartley was one of the oarmen in the first boat to reach the whale. They pulled swiftly, silently on the oars. The harpooner waited at the bow. Then, as they drew alongside the whale, the harpooner sent the harpoon flying.

Immediately the seamen began back oaring to reach clear water. A blow from the massive tail of the whale would shatter the small whale boat.

Suddenly the line went slack. The whale surfaced under the boat. The blow threw the men into the air and shattered the boat. Another longboat picked them up, but James Bartley wasn't found. The others thought he had drowned.

The men aboard *The Star of the East* searched the water all day, waiting for the wounded whale to come up for air. Just at sundown, the dying whale floated to the surface. The crew threw new harpoons into the animal and pulled it to the ship.

They had to work fast. The whale was too huge to take aboard the ship, and hot weather and sharks would quickly spoil the meat. The men worked on top of the whale while it still floated in the water. They worked by lantern light, skinning away the thick blubber. A missed step and they would slip into the water. The sharks circled, waiting!

Shortly before midnight, they had sliced away enough of the flesh so that the rest of the whale could be pulled aboard ship. In the flickering lantern light one of the men working with the fleshing shovels noticed movement in the whale's stomach!

He called the ship's doctor. The doctor slit open the stomach. A human foot—still wearing a shoe—became visible. They ripped open the stomach and pulled out James Bartley. He was in pain and unconscious, but he still lived!

He was in a bad way. His skin had been bleached pale white by digestive juices. The captain had to tie him in a bunk to keep him from rolling about. The doctor did what he could—but none of his medical books told how to care for a person who had spent eighteen hours in a whale!

Bartley remained unconscious for two weeks. But he finally came around and explained how it had happened. "I was flung into the air, and as I fell back the whale's tremendous mouth opened. I screamed. I remember fighting for my breath and kicking about—then I fainted dead away."

James Bartley never went to sea again. He went back to his hometown of Gloucester, England, where he became a shoe cobbler. The captain and the doctor, as well as the crew, of *The Star of the East* signed a paper testifying to the fact that he had spent more than eighteen hours in the belly of a whale.

Scientists and medical men came from all over to examine him and ask him more questions about his incredible experience. When he died his tomb carried these words: "James Bartley, a modern Jonah."

Three days in a whale isn't the entire story of Jonah. The Book of Jonah in the Old Testament is only four chapters long, and you can read it yourself in a few minutes. Jonah was a prophet of God who refused to preach to the people of Nineveh because they were Assyrians, enemies of Israel.

The Bible isn't clear what kind of creature swallowed Jonah. Many people believe it was some type of whale. The whale is the largest animal living in the sea. The blue whale grows more than one hundred feet long and has a mouth large enough to hold five men at once. But the Bible says only that Jonah was taken by some kind of sea creature.

The American scientist Peter Farb thinks it might have been the man-eating white shark, which grows to a length of sixty feet. Peter Farb says,

"This shark has the strange ability to store food in its belly for many days without digesting it."

Experts who study the sea can't answer this perplexing question, but they can't deny the story itself. James Bartley lived for eighteen hours in a whale, and he was only a sailor—not a prophet of God.

15

The Clock That Couldn't Keep Time

One of the most dangerous problems facing science and religion today is misunderstanding. People who have knowledge of the Bible, but no grounding in scientific procedures, believe recent scientific discoveries contradict the Bible.

On the other hand, scientists who have not studied the Bible are mistaken about what it says. An example of this is the Ussher Chronology. A chronology is a system of keeping time, like a calendar. Every calendar must have a beginning point. James Ussher choose 4004 B.C. as the beginning point for his chronology because that's when he believed creation took place.

James Ussher was an Irish scholar who wrote numerous books about the Bible. He was an expert in ancient Semitic languages, and he believed there were enough clues in the Bible to establish the date of creation.

He set out to study all references to time in the Old Testament. By carefully listing all the men who are mentioned there, and adding up their ages, he arrived at the date 4004 B.C. for the date when God created the heavens and the earth.

The publishers of the King James Translation were coming out with a new edition of this popular translation, and to increase sales they wanted to add Bible aids to the margin of the new Bible. They decided to use Ussher's dates. Because of this, thousands of readers of the Bible thought these dates were a part of the original text of Scripture. But Ussher's dates are not found in the manuscripts of the Bible.

James Ussher read more into the Bible than was actually there. The same thing has occurred in the world of science. Men have read the calendar of nature and put a date for creation. But they cannot be any more accurate than James Ussher.

Man has always been interested in his past and the history of his long-ago ancestors. But for centuries it has been impossible to determine just how old ancient objects really are. The older they are, the more difficult to tell their ages, even within a few hundred years.

For a long time scientists have looked for a way to date past events accurately. There are two ways to do this: relative and absolute.

In relative dating, past events are arranged in the order in which they occurred in time.

For example, the best-known method of relative dating is layering. An old, broken vase is found in a layer of soil. Several layers above it is a painted piece of pottery. The broken vase is older than the pottery because it is located below the other.

But this method has pitfalls. Burrowing animals cause dislocations. They dig holes, and items in higher layers fall into lower layers. Earthquakes may upset the order of layers. The record becomes jumbled. Relative dating is not very accurate and not very useful.

Absolute dating is much more satisfying. How old is this crude stone ax? When were these Indian dwellings built? How long ago did the potter live who fashioned this clay vase?

If only scientists could answer these questions! For hundreds of years they dreamed of an absolute dating system that worked.

Some ancient civilizations kept written records, and this is the most reliable method for absolute dating of human history. The cuneiform tablets of the Babylonians and the Egyptian Book of Kings have proven themselves a storehouse of history for establishing when events occurred.

But in many parts of the world these old records are lost, and many other ancient languages are difficult or impossible to translate. Until the last few hundred years more than 90 percent of the earth's people could not read or write. These civilizations left no written records.

Until 1948 absolute dates could be established only one time in a thousand. But in 1948 atomic scientists announced the radiocarbon method of dating.

According to the atomic scientists, the carbon-14 method always worked—without fail. All the archaeologists needed was something from the digging site that contained carbon, such as bones, wood, charcoal, or shells.

Radioactive carbon-14 is continuously formed in the atmosphere as cosmic rays strike regular nitrogen atoms and change them into carbon-14 atoms. The radioactive carbon-14 is absorbed, or taken into, living things and becomes a part of their body. When the living thing dies, the absorption of radioactive carbon ends. As the years pass it slowly breaks back down into nonradioactive carbon-12.

The amount of radioactive carbon-14 still remaining in a body slowly grows less and less after it dies. This tells how long ago the specimen died.

The new science of radioactive dating was applied to the old field of archaeology. Archaeologists were not atomic scientists, and they did not fully understand the process. But they welcomed the method as an answer to their dream for accurate absolute dating.

Carbon-14 became the major method of dating

past events. Sometimes it was the only method. If the age was in doubt, then carbon-14 settled the matter, even if the result didn't agree with other ways of dating.

For fifteen years carbon-14 was a bright weapon to push back the cloak of darkness hiding past history. But as archaeologists used the carbon-14 method, they became more and more disturbed.

Problems came up. A Spanish institute dated one piece of ancient wood at five thousand years. A laboratory in France gave the same piece of wood an age of forty-five hundred years. Later the University of California conducted tests and found the age at seventeen hundred years, while the University of Pennsylvania put the age at only twelve hundred years.

On another occasion, archaeologists accurately dated by several different methods a piece of wood from an Egyptian tomb. They put the age at forty-five hundred years. The wood was tested by carbon-14. Carbon-14 missed the true age by five hundred years.

Scientific American, one of the most widely read scientific journals, recently reported about careful tests made on the California bristlecone pine, the earth's oldest living thing. These tests show that the carbon-14 content in tree rings has varied because of changes in the amount of cosmic-ray bombardment of the atmosphere. For this reason an entire new "time-line" must be worked out. Dates from 1400 B.C. must be adjusted by as much as seven hundred years.

The puzzling errors can also be caused by substances in the soil and sulfuric gases from volcanos. Regardless of the reason, scientists no longer blindly suggest that carbon-14 is completely accurate as they did a few years ago. The carbon-14 clock may run—but it doesn't keep good time.

16

The Man Who Never Was

The strange case of the Piltdown Man began in 1908 when Charles Dawson walked along a country lane in Piltdown Commons, Sussex, England. He was a country lawyer and an amateur archaeologist.

He stopped to watch a road crew working in a gravel pit between the road and the hedge around Barkham Manor. They threw out a reddish object and Dawson picked it up. "What's this?" he asked a workman.

"A coconut, sir," the workman said.

Dawson disagreed. "Stop! It's part of a skull." He examined the gravel pit and found two bone fragments from the top of a skull. He continued digging after the workmen left and found seven more tiny pieces of the skull.

The lawyer took the bones home to examine them more closely. Iron oxide in the soil had stained them dark brown. He soaked the fragile remains in potassium dichromate to preserve them.

Dawson took the pieces of the skull to Dr. Arthur Smith Woodward, Keeper of the Department of Geology at the British Museum. The skull immediately interested Woodward. It appeared very old.

Woodward and Dawson returned to the gravel pit and searched for other parts of the skeleton. They came across an extremely peculiar looking jawbone in about the same place the skull had been found. The jawbone seemed to belong to the same skeleton, but in contrast to the human upper skull, it looked like an ape's jaw. On the other hand, the jaw had teeth shaped like human teeth.

Woodward was so excited about the discovery he failed to notice that the jawbone had been stained not only with iron oxide like the skull, but also by potassium dichromate. Dawson had soaked the skull bones in potassium dichromate *after* he had dug them up, but the jaw bone had been stained with potassium dichromate *before* it was dug up.

Had Dawson worked with the jawbone before he and Woodward found it in the gravel pit? Strangely, no scientist wondered about this question.

The strange shape of the jaw convinced Woodward that the skeleton had belonged to a being half man, half ape. Another English scientist, Sir Arthur Keith, an expert on the brain, said, "The skull represents an extremely ancient form of man. It is the most primitive human brain so far uncovered."

But one British scientist disagreed. He studied the Piltdown bones. Matching the jaw and skull together couldn't be done. "It's like linking a chimpanzee's foot to the bones of a human leg. They simply do not fit." An American zoologist, G. S. Miller, declared, "Except for the teeth, the jawbone is like that of a modern orangutan."

Woodward and Keith quickly slapped down these objections. Couldn't the jaw and skull have been washed together accidentally? "No!" they cried. Apes had not lived in England until recent times. The skull and jawbone were very ancient; they must belong together.

Woodward gave the Piltdown Man the scientific name *Eoanthropus dawsoni*, which means Dawson's Dawn man. They believed Piltdown

Man had fallen into an old river, had been washed downstream along with the gravel, and finally had come to rest in a quiet eddy which later became the gravel pit.

But Woodward and Sir Arthur Keith couldn't agree on how the skull and jaw fitted together. The point of attachment was missing and it couldn't be found in the gravel pit. Woodward calculated the brain capacity to be about 1100 cubic centimeters, while Arthur Keith believed the brain size to be about 1500 cubic centimeters.

The two men got together and decided to avoid debate by listing the brain capacity at 1350 cubic centimeters. This is the average size of an adult human being.

They searched the gravel pit again. This time they uncovered a curving bone club which had been sharpened on one end and pierced with a hole at the other. Did this club belong to Piltdown Man?

Up until that time, all of the ancient bones discovered had either definitely belonged to an ape, or definitely belonged to a man. This was the only skeleton that appeared to be a mixture of both. The crude bone club settled the matter—only man makes and uses tools.

The new discovery burst upon the scientific world like a thunderbolt. The Piltdown Man was reconstructed and published in scientific journals and textbooks. Museums throughout the world put plaster casts of the Piltdown skull on display.

The British Museum proudly displayed the Piltdown skull with the words "Dawn Man" gleaming over the glass case. Scientists came from all over the world to view it.

The 1926 edition of the *Encyclopaedia Britannica* devoted an entire article to the skull. The encyclopaedia said scientists at first thought the bones had fallen together accidentally, but now "they have disposed of that idea."

But forty years after its discovery, the Piltdown Man was proven to never have existed! In 1949, Kenneth P. Oakley showed that the entire discovery was a hoax.

Other scientists had worked with plaster casts of the bones; but Oakley went back to the actual bones. First, he used fluorine dating to determine the age. Because fluorine slowly soaks into bones, the older a bone is the more fluorine it contains.

He took a few splinters of bone from the skull and from the jaw and compared their ages with that of a bone from a modern chimpanzee. His tests showed that all three were the same age. Piltdown Man wasn't old after all!

Next he looked at the color of the bones. All were reddish in color due to iron oxide action. But the color was only surface deep. A truly old bone would have been stained through and through.

Backing up this discovery was the odd fact that the bones still contained collagen fibers easily visible with a microscope. These fibers are only found in bones a few hundred years old at most.

The bone club? Oakley showed that it had come from an elephant leg bone. It had been whittled with a steel knife and stained to look old.

The teeth of Piltdown Man were black, but Oakley found that the color could be scraped away. The black substance was paint! Underneath, the teeth still gleamed white.

The teeth showed heavy signs of wear—like human teeth. Monkeys eat tender shoots of grass and fruit which do not wear their teeth. But in the Piltdown jaw the monkey teeth had been deliberately filed down to make them look human.

The skull had come from a modern man, the jaw from a modern orangutan.

Oakley said, "The archaeologists who took part in the excavations at Piltdown were the victims of a most elaborate and carefully prepared hoax."

The fraud should have been easy to detect. The greatest scientists in England had examined Piltdown Man, and they should have spotted the deception.

Kenneth P. Oakley's paper touched off a wild uproar. The British Parliament demanded an investigation. Scientists who had defended Piltdown Man tried to hide their red faces. They refused to speak to reporters. The painful hoax caused a terrible scandal. At first, Sir Arthur Keith refused to believe that he had been fooled so easily.

Who pulled the hoax? No one knows. Charles Dawson died in 1916; those who knew him said he was an honest man. Yet, no one else around Piltdown Commons had the skill to fix the bones to make them look old.

Today scientists are more careful when they speak of man's past. There are too many blanks, too many unsolved puzzles. And over it all is the embarrassing mistake of the Piltdown Man—the man who never was.

17

Hoax from Down Under

The platypus is a sleek-furred little animal living in eastern Australia. It is the strangest of all creatures. This puzzling patchwork has the thick fur and flat tail of a beaver, the bill and webbed feet of a duck, the sharp spurs of a rooster, and the poison of a snake.

The mother platypus lays eggs and hatches them like a bird, but she feeds her young with milk like other mammals. Finally, the platypus barks like a dog!

Many of the strange animals of Australia were discovered in 1629 when a Dutch ship commanded by Captain Palsaert wrecked off shore. Captain Palsaert and his crew waded ashore. They saw the kangaroo and the koala bear.

After their rescue they described the animals they had seen, but because their descriptions were so peculiar scientists dismissed their stories. Captain Palsaert and his crew must have been suffering from delusions caused by the shipwreck!

More than a hundred years passed before scientists studied the kangaroo, the koala, and other animals of Australia. But another surprise awaited them!

An explorer sent the dried skin of an animal to Dr. George Shaw, who worked for the British Museum in London. But this animal, with the fur of a beaver, had the bill of a duck!

The scientists at the British Museum declared the stuffed animal a clever fake. Dr. Shaw thought some joker had grafted the bill of a duck onto the body of a small animal. He even tried to pry off the bill. The skin is still on display at the British Museum, and the marks of his scissors can be seen.

A mammal with the bill of a duck was bad enough, but the local people of Australia reported that the platypus laid eggs instead of giving birth to live young.

This wouldn't do! The platypus didn't fit into the scientists' scheme of things. Clearly the platypus was a mammal. It had hair and fur and the four-chambered heart of other mammals, such as the beaver. It was warm blooded, and the mother platypus provided milk for the young. Yet who ever heard of a mammal laying eggs!

The platypus simply couldn't exist. It must be a hoax! Besides, scientists had been to Australia to study other animals, but they had never seen a platypus alive.

They didn't know that the platypus is an incredibly shy creature. Its home is a burrow in the bank of a stream. After dark it slides out of the burrow and into the water. It is both semi-aquatic and nocturnal. This means that the platypus spends much of its time in the water, and it usually comes out only at night. No wonder the scientists missed it.

Scientists called the animal *Paradoxis*—a paradox, something that doesn't make sense. In 1884, W. H. Caldwell sailed to Australia to settle the argument about the platypus.

Caldwell found a living platypus and studied its daily life. He found the bill wasn't hard like a duck's bill. Instead, the platypus had a soft bill with sensitive nerves along the surface.

When the platypus slides into the dark, muddy waters where it feeds, a flap of skin covers his eyes and ears. But the sensitive bill makes it possible for him to nuzzle through the mud and feel out worms, grubs, and water insects.

The bill serves another purpose. The nostrils are near the end of the bill. The platypus can remain hidden under water and breathe with only the tip of his bill exposed.

The platypus looks ungainly on the land, but once it dips below the surface of the water, it becomes a well-designed swimmer. The gray fur is thick and sleek, the powerful front feet are webbed, and its flat tail is a rudder for fast turns.

All through the night it feeds. The platypus stuffs crayfish into its mouth. At dawn it crawls into the grasslined nest, and then eats the crayfish stored in its cheeks.

Male and female look alike, but there is one definite way to tell a male. He has a spur on each hind leg. This horny spur connects to a poison gland. The poison is similar to the poison of a snake.

The male duckbill is the only mammal that can be called venomous. A fisherman was the first to find this out when he caught a platypus on his hook, and tried to release it. The platypus stabbed him with the spur. The fisherman ended up in the hospital, but he recovered. Since then other people have been poisoned, but no one has died.

Slowly, W. H. Caldwell discovered these facts. After months of patient studying, Caldwell found a den made far back into the bank of a stream.

The mother platypus had hollowed out a roomy chamber. She had a tunnel entrance from under the water, and another small tunnel to the surface. This served as a pipe to let in fresh air.

The mother platypus lined her nest with leaves and shredded grass. In the nest she laid two soft-shelled eggs. Each egg was about the size of a grape—about the size of pigeon eggs.

Instead of sitting on the eggs, the platypus curled around them. The eggs hatched in ten days. The two young animals were blind, without fur, and completely helpless. But they grew strong on their mother's milk, and after four months they could care for themselves. The little creatures rolled and tumbled together like little puppies.

W. H. Caldwell returned to England and spoke to the scientists about his discoveries. The platypus was a real animal, and not a hoax put together by pranksters in Australia.

The delegates of the British Association for the Advancement of Science rose to their feet in wild cheering. Finally, it was settled! The strange animal from Australia was as wonderfully strange as the explorers had said.

The Bible says that God created all the living creatures on the earth. We cannot help but be amazed at the many wonderful animals that He has put on the earth.

18

The Fish That Couldn't Be

Miss Courtenay Latimer was a serious young woman who worked for the local museum in East London, South Africa. Although the museum had been established to display historical items from the area, she wanted to expand the museum by adding fish from the ocean to the collection.

The director of the museum, Dr. Bruce-Bays, didn't think much of her idea. The museum didn't have money for purchasing fish.

But East London was a fishing port, and Miss Latimer knew that many of the fish caught couldn't be sold as food. She thought she could talk the local fishing captains into donating unusual fish to the museum rather than throwing them over the side.

On December 22, 1938, Captain Goosen called her aboard his ship. He had caught a mysterious fish five feet long. It was a real monster in appearance. The scales were steel-blue, and the powerful jaws had vicious teeth.

December is the peak of the summer season in the Southern Hemisphere, and the heat had already caused the fascinating fish with the strange body to spoil.

Miss Latimer hired a taxi to carry the smelly passenger to the museum. There she searched through books for the name of the peculiar fish. None of the books had anything like this. "It must be very rare," she said. "I'll preserve it."

Director Bruce-Bays disagreed. The oily fish didn't fit into the refrigerator, and the museum couldn't afford to build a tank and fill it with formalin, a preservative. No, they couldn't keep the fish.

The fishy odor grew stronger and stronger. Something had to be done.

Miss Latimer sketched a drawing and had a friend take photographs of the creature. Immediately she mailed the sketches and a written description to Dr. James Smith, the world-famous authority on African fishes at Rhodes University. He had discovered one hundred new fishes himself.

Dr. James Smith read her letter. He could not believe his eyes. What she had drawn was a *coelacanth*.

According to the timetable of scientists the last of the coelacanths had died out more than sixty million years ago. Dr. Smith later said, "If I had seen a dinosaur walking down the street I would not have been as surprised."

This was impossible. Dr. James Smith could only believe some mistake had been made. He wrote to Miss Latimer and asked her to send the photographs.

Alas! The pictures were fogged. She sent him two of the rough fish scales, but the slimy body was too spoiled to ship. Instead, she loaded the coelacanth in a wheel barrow and pushed it to the local taxidermist to be mounted.

She wrote to Dr. Smith and begged him to come and see for himself. "The fish does exist," she said. "The taxidermist has him."

Dr. James Smith arrived twelve days later. He rushed into the museum in his rumpled field clothes. He had driven three hundred miles over primitive roads. He was tired, dirty, and desperately sleepy. But he had to see the fish!

Director Bruce-Bays had never been interested in

the oily fish with its weird set of fins. He believed Miss Latimer had become too excited. And this man certainly didn't look like a great scientist.

Dr. Smith felt the sharp teeth, rubbed its tough scales, poked the fleshy fins, and tapped the bare, armored head.

"It is a *coelacanth* all right," he said. "Miss Latimer, you've made the most important discovery in the study of fish during this century. I'll call this species *latimeria* in appreciation of what you have done."

Other scientists refused to believe the catch. Some suggested that the fish had been frozen for all those years and then thawed out to be caught in Captain Goosen's fishing net. Others believed the whole thing a hoax.

"No," Miss Latimer said. "Captain Goosen said this one lived for several hours after he brought it up in his net along with some sharks."

"Then there must be others," Dr. James Smith declared.

Dr. Smith examined the fish. Its blue color told him that the coelacanth lived at a depth of about 250 feet. Deeper than that the fish were usually black in color. The fact that it had been caught with sharks confirmed that the coelacanth didn't live at too great a depth.

The stubby body and short fins probably meant it couldn't swim very fast. "It probably lurks among rocks, concealed by its bluish color, and swoops out to catch other fish as food. Once caught in those sharp teeth, nothing could escape."

Somehow the fish had survived for centuries without being caught in a net. Dr. Smith didn't want to wait a hundred years for another coelacanth.

He printed a "wanted" poster describing the fish and offered a four-hundred-dollar reward for its capture dead or alive. He asked help from the fishing boats off the island of Madagascar. He believed the coelacanth made its home in the rocks around that island.

Fourteen long years passed without a report of another coelacanth being caught. Most scientists put aside the single specimen of Miss Latimer's as a freak.

In 1952, on Christmas Eve, Dr. Smith received a cable from Captain Eric Hunt who fished off the coast of Zanzibar. "Have coelacanth," the telegraph read. "Come and fetch it."

Dr. Smith was pleased at first, then he immediately became worried. The fish was two thousand miles away. The telegram had taken four days to reach him. Would the fish still be in good condition?

He ordered Captain Hunt to freeze the fish, inject formalin into it or salt it down. Do something to preserve it!

Dr. Smith was beside himself with excitement. He did not have enough money to charter a boat to fetch the fish. He appealed to Prime Minister Daniel F. Malan for help.

The prime minister was amused by this scientist who wanted a plane to haul a fish, but he understood the urgency after Dr. Smith explained. He ordered an army airplane to fly the fish scientist to the new catch.

It was another coelacanth!

While he was there Dr. Smith interviewed the local natives. He asked if they had seen the fish before.

"Yes," one man said. "I've cooked them for

food—they need a lot of salt." Someone else added that the scales could be used for sandpaper.

The coelacanth turned out to be more common than at first believed. Since 1952, sixty more of the ancient fish have been caught and preserved.

The discovery of living coelacanths is regarded as the most amazing event of the century in the realm of natural history.

19

Rocks from the Sky

Almost two hundred years ago people had the curious notion that rocks fell from the sky. "Impossible!" the scientists of that time said. "Where do the rocks fall from? Do they drop from the clouds? Such an idea is nothing but the imagination of superstitious country folk."

When European settlers came to the New World they discovered Aztec Indians of South America with tools and knives made of iron. But the Aztecs didn't have the skill necessary for extracting iron from iron ore. Where did the iron come from? The Aztecs explained that rocks containing pure iron fell from the sky. They prized the metal more than gold.

The French Academy, a powerful and respected group of scientists, completely discounted the falling-rock reports. Once, an old French priest came to the Paris Museum with a stone which he described as having fallen from the sky.

"No," the museum curator said. "You must be mistaken. You should know better. Rocks can't fall from the sky because there are none up there to fall."

The priest asked the academy to investigate anyway. A committee of several respected chemists and geologists studied the rocks. They replied, "We regret that in our enlightened age there still are people so superstitious as to believe stones fall from the sky. This peculiar-looking stone is nothing more than soil which has been struck by lightning."

Many museum directors read the academy's report and searched through their geology displays. They had many blackened stones that had been donated by people who claimed to have seen the objects streak through the night sky like a flash of lightning and crash with an ear-shattering bang. The museum directors removed the scorched rocks and hid them out of sight.

The truth about the falling stones became known in Europe on April 16, 1803. During broad daylight on a clear day, three thousand stones fell in a single shower. The French Academy was meeting only seventy-five miles away. More than three hundred people testified to the truth. This time there was no doubt. Stones do fall from the sky!

In America, however, the truth didn't come as quickly.

In 1807, Benjamin Stilliman, an American chemist, saw such an object fall. He reported to the president of the United States, Thomas Jefferson, who was an amateur scientist. The professor invited President Jefferson to come to the field and see for himself the stone which had buried itself upon impact.

President Jefferson declined the invitation. "I find it easier to believe that a Yankee professor would lie than that stones would fall from heaven."

Stilliman investigated further. He discovered many honest and dependable people who backed him up. The people claimed they had found rocks that were still hot enough to blister their fingers. Finally, Stilliman wrote a book describing the fiery objects. Most American scientists did not believe him.

But rocks did fall from the sky. They still do! The objects come from space and are called meteorites by today's scientists. We call them "shooting stars."

It wasn't until November 12, 1833, that everyone in the United States became convinced of the existence of meteorites. A southern cotton plantation owner awoke to the cries of horror from the household. "The world is on fire!" they cried.

When he ran outside, he saw a spectacle which is only seen once or twice in five hundred years. That night millions of shooting stars appeared to light the sky with long streaks.

He said, "Never did rain fall thicker than the meteors fall toward the earth: East, west, north, and south it was the same."

It continued all night all across the United States. People ran into the streets. They thought the sky was falling. But when after a few hours nothing had happened, the people began to enjoy the splendid display. It was better than the fireworks on a Fourth of July.

Most of the meteors never reached the earth that night. They burned to ash and the ash drifted to the ground. In places where snow covered the ground, the ash could be seen as a layer that spotted the snow. A few of the meteors did strike the earth and were found. After the display which was witnessed by the whole nation, the scientists had to admit that the impossible did happen. Rocks could fall from the sky.

A "shooting star" is called a meteoroid while still in space. As it lights up when slamming into the earth's atmosphere it is called a meteor. If it reaches the ground, then it is a meteorite.

Although scientists accepted meteorites as actual objects, very few studied them. One astronomer said, "Once the meteor enters the atmosphere I lose all interest in it."

Geologists, on the other hand, pointed out that they studied the earth. Meteorites were from space and did not come under their study.

This is how things stood when Harvey H. Nininger entered the state college in Oklahoma in the 1920s. He had grown up in the Oklahoma cotton fields, and at first he was fearful of his ability to succeed in college. Within a few months, however, he found himself at the head of his science class. He graduated from the college with honors and was asked to stay on as a teacher.

One night as he walked home he saw a fireball. This caused him to become interested in meteorites, but when he looked for books about meteorites he was surprised at how little information had been printed on the subject. He asked astronomy professors at the college about meteorites. To his surprise he learned that they had not heard a single lecture on the subject.

He talked to geology professors and discovered the same thing. They had never seen a meteorite, although they knew the names and chemical composition of thousands of common minerals and rocks.

Nininger set out to collect and study meteorites. Within a few years he had become the foremost authority on shooting stars. He developed a system to plot their path and find the impact point. He paid farmers one dollar a pound for meteorites that landed in their fields.

He was appalled and challenged at the lack of interest astronomers had in meteorites. "Here," he said, "are the only pieces of material that come from outside the earth." He lectured to anybody who would listen to him: farmers, school children, store owners, college professors, anybody!

He would hand them a piece of meteorite. "In

your two hands you are holding a piece of matter from outer space!"

Finding meteorites is a difficult task. They can come at any time from any direction. They strike the atmosphere at twenty thousand miles per hour, or even faster. The friction from the earth's atmosphere causes the meteor to heat to a temperature of ten thousand degrees Fahrenheit. It's a short life thereafter. The air ahead of the speeding object glows momentarily and a tail of white-hot molten rock produces a glowing trail that can be seen for hundreds of miles.

Shooting stars are caused by small stones, usually no bigger than peas. Most of the tiny stones are completely destroyed fifty miles above the earth. A very, very few are large enough to survive the plunge earthward. These large meteorites slow to a leisurely three hundred miles per hour and bury themselves in a shallow crater a few feet deep.

There are two kinds of meteorites. The most common is the granite type which is similar to stones found on earth except for the outer layer which is blackened. The second type is iron. Both types are difficult to recover from a field. The stony type looks like ordinary stone, while the iron meteorite will rust away when left in the soil for long periods of time.

Several thousand years ago a huge meteorite weighing several tons failed to lose its tremendous speed and continued to bore into the atmosphere at thirty thousand miles per hour. Some of the material burned away, but the remaining part finally struck the ground. The explosion created a large crater almost a mile across and more than six hundred feet deep. The crater is near Winslow, Arizona.

Nininger's lectures paid off. More and more people wrote to him telling of meteoric falls. In 1940 he opened his own museum near the famous meteorite crater in Arizona.

Soon after Nininger opened his meteoric museum, aircraft manufacturers began work on the proper shape for jet planes. At the time most engineers believed high-speed aircraft should be needle nosed.

Nininger disagreed. "Needle-nosed aircraft will not fly straight and level. At extremely high speeds heat will melt the needle." He proposed that high speed aircraft have a blunt nose.

He showed the aircraft designers a meteorite that had managed to survive the fiery plunge through the atmosphere. It had a blunt nose. He suggested the engineers try his meteorite in a wind tunnel test. They turned down his suggestion.

During the next five years, well-designed aircraft suddenly became uncontrollable at high speeds. The heat build-up became unacceptable.

As the years passed the blunt nose became more and more acceptable. By the time of the moon flights, the Apollo command module was protected by a blunt-shaped heat shield as it reentered the earth's atmosphere.

There are many unanswered questions about meteorites. Where in space do they begin their journey to earth? Why do they travel at such high speeds? Why do they come in bunches? Why are some made of rock and others of iron?

Many of the answers are still hidden in the rocks found by Nininger in farmers' fields. All in all he has recovered more outer-space rocks than the astronauts brought back from the moon.

20

The Musician Who Discovered a Planet

His friends laughed when William Herschel told them he wanted to become an astronomer. "You're a musician," they said. "Leave the planets to the astronomers at Greenwich. They are the experts."

It was true. The observatory at Greenwich had many fine telescopes made by experts and used by great astronomers.

William Herschel lived at Bath, England, a resort town on the Avon River. There he composed music and taught students, played in the orchestra and led the choir of the famous Octagon Chapel and played the organ. He became conductor of the orchestra, but he kept his many other duties, too.

"You don't have a telescope," his friend reminded him.

That was true, too. A good telescope to view the planets cost more than William Herschel could afford.

Each night before he went to sleep, William Herschel read in bed with the covers pulled up to keep him warm. Around him in a tumbled heap were books on music, mathematics, optics, and astronomy. He read about Saturn with its strange rings, Mars with its red surface and white ice caps, Venus with its brilliant white clouds.

Finally he saved enough to rent a telescope for three months. Just three months! Herschel used the little telescope every clear night. Even during the intermission when he led the concert and was dressed in the fancy clothes of a conductor, he would jump over the hedge behind the concert hall and run across the cobblestone street to his home. There the telescope waited, set up in his garden ready to be used.

When the time came to return the telescope, his friends thought he would be satisfied. "Now he will leave the planets to the astronomers," they said.

But William Herschel wasn't satisfied. He wanted a telescope of his own. A bigger, better telescope than the one he had rented.

"If I can't buy one, then I'll make one," he resolved.

The first telescope he made wasn't as good as he had hoped, but it was better than no telescope at all. He didn't give up. His sister Caroline read to him as he worked for as long as sixteen hours at a time. She fed him as he worked. He made more than two hundred telescopes before he finished one that suited him.

What should he study with his new telescope? Planets? No, professional astronomers with their excellent telescopes studied the planets. That left the stars.

"I intend to examine all the stars that can be seen in my telescope," he decided.

Herschel's telescope made the planets and moon seem two hundred times larger. The stars were so far away, so very far away, that through a telescope, even a modern telescope, they still appear as tiny points of light.

Herschel swept the sky and examined each star. Caroline kept notes for him. Some stars are very bright, others are extremely dim. Some are deep red, others are bright blue. Some even change in brightness—they are blinking lights. Some stars come in pairs, triplets, and even huge clusters of many thousands.

Herschel hunted out these strange sights. His sky survey took four years. During that time, he discovered two thousand double stars and twenty-five hundred star clusters.

Still, most people thought it was a waste of time. What could Herschel discover of importance that wasn't already known to other astronomers? Although he spent as much time with his telescope as he did with his music students, he was still considered a musician.

All of this changed Tuesday night, March 13, 1781. Herschel pointed his telescope to a dim star in the constellation of Taurus, the Bull. When he looked through the eyepiece the star was a fuzzy ball.

That wasn't right. Stars should be sharp points of light. Herschel tried a higher power. The object became bigger. This certainly couldn't be a star!

Herschel wondered. It might be a comet. Or, maybe a planet!

It was a new planet. Only five planets were known. Here was a new one. Herschel's planet, named Uranus, was four times the size of earth. And an amateur astronomer using a homemade telescope set up in his garden discovered it.

Professional astronomers went back over their records. Uranus is just barely visible to the naked eye, and astronomers had observed it seventeen times before, but no one recognized it as a planet. John Flamsteed, the first Astronomer Royal in England, had actually recorded it as a star on one of his star maps, but a hundred years passed and no one caught his mistake.

Astronomers came to visit Herschel and to look through his telescope. They marveled at the telescope and begged him to make telescopes for their observatories.

The Royal Society invited him to become a member. "Come to Greenwich Observatory," they said. "Bring your telescope!"

There is a strange postscript to the story of Uranus.

Fifty years after William Herschel discovered Uranus, astronomers became disturbed with the planet's movement. They had followed it carefully from year to year. By using Newton's law of gravitation, they could calculate its orbit. But Uranus did not follow the path they predicted. Something was wrong. What could be causing Uranus to change its course?

Some astronomers didn't believe there was a problem at all. Uranus had gone astray by only a tiny amount. This could be due to poor observations or experimental error. But the years passed and Uranus moved farther and farther off course. This large error couldn't be explained away.

George Biddell Airy, the new Astronomer Royal of England, put forward another explanation. He believed the great distance of Uranus from the sun caused the problem. Gravity at that great distance didn't work the same way it did on nearby planets such as the earth.

A few astronomers thought the change in orbit of Uranus might be due to another planet farther out from the sun. When Uranus passed near the unseen planet it would be pulled out of its orbit by the gravitational attraction.

One of the people who believed that another planet, as yet undiscovered, orbited farther out was John Couch Adams in England.

John Couch Adams had won a scholarship to Cambridge University because of his mathematical ability. It was quite an honor because he had grown up in poverty on a farm. While in college he took extra work tutoring students to send money to his parents.

In his spare time he set to work trying to figure out where a planet would have to be to cause the changes observed in Uranus's orbit. Such calculations are extremely difficult. After two years he had an answer which gave the position and size of the unknown planet.

He was still a student at Cambridge when he sent the results of his calculations to George Airy.

The Astronomer Royal was in many ways a small-minded man, sure of his own intelligence, and unable to recognize important ideas when they came from other people. He ran the observatory at Greenwich like a dictator. Any research with the telescope had to be personally approved by him.

The letter from the young mathematics student arrived. George Airy looked it over. He still believed a breakdown in Newton's law of gravitation at great distances caused the unexplained motions of Uranus—not a planet further out.

In any case, he thought it impossible for an unknown student to predict the position of an unseen planet with pen-and-paper calculations. He tossed aside the letter from John Adams. Airy refused to waste telescope time searching for the planet.

Six months passed.

Unknown to John Adams, a French astronomer named Joseph Leverrier had worked out the same problem. He, too, arrived at an answer, exactly the same answer as the English mathematics student.

Airy saw Leverrier's report. He became alarmed that there might be something after all. In a panic he ordered a search be made with the telescope.

But he made another wrong decision. He thought the new planet would be too remote to look like anything except a star. He instructed the telescope observer to plot every star on a star chart rather than scanning the area for a suspicious object.

Johann Galle at the Berlin Observatory in Germany pointed his telescope at the spot predicted by Adams and Leverrier. On September 23, 1846, he opened the observatory dome, and within thirty minutes he found the planet.

Later, astronomers found old star charts which showed that they had seen the planet upon several occasions, but they had failed to recognize it as a planet.

Although Johann Galle of Germany was the first person to see the planet, later called Neptune, Joseph Leverrier and John Adams are given credit for the discovery.

The Astronomer Royal, George Airy, is remembered, too. Although George Airy made many important discoveries, including a way to make eyeglasses which correct for astigmatic vision, he is remembered for his great failure. Airy is the astronomer who lost a planet.

21

Star's Fingerprints

Joseph von Fraunhofer wiped sweat from his forehead with the cuff of his stained shirt. He placed another clay pot on the tray and slid it into the furnace. In the Bavarian city of Straubing in 1799 it was common for young people to work at factories to help support the family.

Fraunhofer had hoped to study science, but his family was poor. When he was only twelve years old he dropped out of school and began work as a glazier in a pottery factory. Unless something happened he would spend the rest of his life feeding clay bowls and vases into the glazing furnace.

Something did happen. The family lived in an old, sagging apartment building. One day the two-story building fell down. Fraunhofer was trapped inside. Workmen began a frantic effort to rescue the boy. They had little hope of finding him alive.

People gathered to watch. A wealthy optician who owned the Utzschneider optical institute found his carriage blocked by the workmen digging through the rubble. He decided to wait to see the outcome.

It was Fraunhofer's lucky day, although he didn't know it at the time. The workmen found him alive. They persuaded the wealthy optician to use his carriage to carry the boy to the doctor.

The doctor checked Fraunhofer over and explained that the only thing the boy needed was a good meal. The wealthy optician took Fraunhofer to his mansion and nursed him back to health.

Until that moment, Fraunhofer had not been interested in astronomy or telescopes. He knew nothing of stars, and he had never met an astronomer. He wasn't even sure of what an optician did.

An optician, his wealthy friend explained, is a person who designs and builds optical instruments such as telescopes and spectroscopes to be used by astronomers.

The color of a star is a clue to its temperature. A yellow star is probably the same temperature as the sun because the sun is yellow, too. Red stars are probably cooler than the sun, while blue-white ones are hotter.

The optician noticed that Fraunhofer was a quick-witted boy, fast to learn and willing to work. He gave Fraunhofer a job at the institute. Fraunhofer would help build the telescopes that astronomers used.

Joseph Fraunhofer read all he could about the great astronomers and their discoveries.

One person he read about was Sir Isaac Newton, the English scientist. In 1666 Newton made one of his first important discoveries. At that time Newton was a college student. During a vacation at his mother's home he used a prism to study the colors of sunlight.

The experiment was simple. He darkened a room and cut a hole in the window curtain to let in a tiny beam of sunlight. A triangular piece of glass, called a prism, caught the sunlight and spread it into the colors of the rainbow. He placed another prism after the first and recombined the colors.

Years later, when astronomers had telescopes which could collect enough starlight, they tried the same experiment. Starlight also spread into the colors. This convinced them that stars are like the sun, but much dimmer and further away.

Most astronomers studied the planets. "The stars

are too remote. We'll never learn anything of them. It's hopeless to attack their secrets."

Joseph Fraunhofer proved himself at the telescope factory. He made many important discoveries, and he was promoted many times. While still a young man he was put in charge of the entire factory.

One instrument he made was a special prism to spread sunlight into its colors. This instrument fitted onto a telescope and was called a spectroscope.

The prisms Fraunhofer made for the spectroscopes were the best in the world.

Before delivering a spectroscope to a new owner, he would set it up in his laboratory and test it out. It was while checking out his latest spectroscope that he made his most important discovery.

He saw tiny black lines along the sun's spectrum. The lines were spaced at irregular intervals all up and down the band of sunlight. At first he feared a defective prism caused the dark bands. But careful study showed that the strange lines were in the sun's spectrum and in the spectrum of starlight.

He wrote to scientists telling them of the lines, but they couldn't see them. Slight imperfections in poorer prisms caused the sharp lines to fuzz out and become invisible.

Scientists scorned him as a mere technician—he had not been educated at a great university. He attended scientific meetings, but scientists refused to let him speak.

Fraunhofer mapped six hundred of the strange lines, but fifty years passed before scientists looking at his reports saw the true meaning of the lines.

They found that each chemical element on earth could be heated until it glowed. When light from the glowing substance is observed in the spectroscope a pattern of lines is produced.

Sodium, for example, has two lines close together. This pattern is easy to spot. No other substance produces lines with exactly the same pattern. Each substance has its own fingerprint. If some unknown substance is heated until it glows, and these two lines appear in the spectrum, then sodium must be part of the unknown substance.

It was a powerful discovery. Each substance could be identified by its fingerprint.

Astronomers studied the spectrum of the sun. They checked off each pattern of lines they found there with patterns of elements found on earth. In that way scientists found that the sun contained hydrogen, carbon, nitrogen, and other elements.

One pattern of lines in the sun's spectrum could not be matched with any element on earth. Here was a substance that existed in the sun but not on the earth. The new substance was named helium, which means "from the sun."

Twenty-five years after the discovery of helium, geologists working at an oil well captured a gas similar to hydrogen. This gas when heated had a spectrum pattern like no other earthly substance. Then the spectrum of the unknown gas was compared with the lines produced by helium found only on the sun. The spectrum lines were the same! Helium had been discovered on the sun before being discovered on earth!

Fraunhofer never became a full-time astronomer. But his discovery of lines in the spectrum suddenly opened the entire universe to astronomers.

22

Impossible Flight

Only five people turned out on the cold, wind-swept slopes of Kill Devil Hill near Kitty Hawk, North Carolina, to watch the Wright brothers attempt the first powered and controlled flight of a heavier-than-air machine.

No scientists or reporters came. After all, Dr. Samuel P. Langley, the scientist in charge of the Smithsonian Institution had worked for six years trying to build a flying machine, and he had failed. He spent fifty thousand dollars to make three machines. He launched the airplanes from the top of a houseboat on the Potomac River. Each time the airplanes crashed into the water.

Simon Newcomb, a professional mathematician and president of the American Astronomical Society, said, "No possible combination of known forms of machinery can be united to form a practical machine by which man shall fly long distances through the air."

Men had watched birds for years and had dreamed of human flight. Some strapped on large, birdlike wings and jumped from cliffs to experience the thrill of soaring. But all experimenters came across two problems. They didn't have a lightweight engine to power the aircraft, and they didn't have a way to control the airplane and keep it balanced during flight.

Otto Lilienthal, a high school student in Germany, constructed a glider with wings like those of the birds. He didn't flap his wings. Instead, Lilienthal tried to change direction by shifting his weight, sliding right and left on the frame. He made two thousand successful glides before a gust of wind tipped his birdlike glider so far he couldn't recover. He died in the crash.

Alexander Graham Bell, the inventor of the telephone, became interested in flying machines. He set up a laboratory in his summer home in Nova Scotia and experimented with large man-carrying kites. He, too, failed to make a successful flying machine.

Orville and Wilbur Wright were self-taught and not well known. Their only claim to fame was the *Wright Special,* a bicycle they made in their bicycle shop in Dayton, Ohio.

Orville and Wilbur decided to distrust everything other flyers had done and begin afresh. They found that there was no really reliable scientific information about flying. They built a wind tunnel to check their design for a flying machine. The wind tunnel let them see how the air flowed over wings. They found many errors in the work done by other scientists who studied flight.

The Wrights built a five-foot model and flew it at the end of a string like a kite. They discovered that the direction of the flight of the model could be controlled by warping the wing tips.

Next they made a man-carrying kite. But the winds around Dayton weren't constant enough for them. They wrote to the Weather Bureau for information about the best site. The Weather Bureau suggested the coast of North Carolina.

When summer ended and the bicycle season slacked off, the brothers packed their things and traveled by train to North Carolina where the breeze from the ocean blew at a constant fifteen miles per hour across the sandy hills.

The site offered good winds, low rolling hills, and no trees to accidentally crash into! But the wind also blew sand into their food, and mosquitoes from nearby marshes flew up in dark clouds. But Orville and Wilbur stuck with the job of flying their kite.

The kite was actually a fifty-two-pound glider with two wings. The cost had been fifteen dollars. This included the cost of sixty yards of white cotton for the wings. They had sewed the cotton to the exact size at home. When they put the glider together in North Carolina, the material slipped down the wings to an exact fit like a tight glove.

At first they kept the airplane tied to the ground with ropes and flew it like a kite. They couldn't keep it under control. It darted suddenly to the right and left. It crashed more than once.

Finally, they developed controls that worked. They cut loose the ropes and took turns making gliding flights. Later, Orville became such an expert glider pilot he stayed in the air for nine minutes, riding along the updraft from the low sand dunes. This record for unpowered flight was not broken for ten years.

The airplane worked! They had an aircraft that would carry a man; they knew how to control it and keep their balance. All they needed was a source of power to replace the wind.

They searched for a motor for their glider. Nowhere could they find one that wasn't too heavy. They solved the problem by building an engine themselves. The four-cylinder water-cooled engine developed twelve horsepower. They carved out the propellers by hand, too.

The time had come to make the first trial.

Shortly before their attempt at powered flight, they read in the *New York Times* an editorial that called Langley's experiments a foolish waste of money and an idle dream. The editorial ended, "Man will not fly for a thousand years."

It was a short thousand years! Ten days later, Orville Wright piloted the *Flyer* a distance of 850 feet. He stayed in the air for almost a minute. On December 17, 1903, at Kitty Hawk, the Wrights made the first successful flight in a full-sized airplane.

When Simon Newcomb heard of the flight he belittled the results. "It's out of the question that their plane might carry the extra weight of a passenger or cargo."

Professor Pickering, an astronomer, said, "There is no hope of competing for racing speed with either our locomotives or our automobiles.

"The popular mind often pictures gigantic flying machines speeding across the Atlantic carrying innumerable passengers in the same way as our modern steamships. It seems safe to say that such an idea is wholly visionary, and the expense would be too much."

Two years later the *Scientific American* magazine still dismissed airplanes as impossible. In fact, the United States government would not consider buying an airplane from the Wrights. They sold their first airplane to France. Then they became a world sensation.

All the scientists had failed. Two self-educated bicycle repair mechanics from Dayton, Ohio, were the first to give wings to man!

23

The Lone Eagle

During the winter of 1926, Charles A. Lindbergh flew an open cockpit airplane carrying mail from Saint Louis to Chicago. The air route didn't have airports. Instead, farmers dotted along the route gave Lindbergh permission to land in their pastures in case of trouble.

Once, during a night flight when fog closed in, Lindbergh couldn't find a landing site. He circled until the engine sputtered, out of gas. He parachuted moments before the airplane crashed.

Lindbergh knew the future of fast transportation depended on aviation. Few people agreed with him. Only the larger cities had airports, and these were nothing more than large grassy fields.

Nevil Shute, a leading engineer, said, "The forecast that passenger-carrying aeroplanes will travel at over 300 miles per hour is impossible. Flying will remain a matter of stunts and thrills."

Charles Lindbergh read in the newspapers about Raymond Oretig, a New York hotel owner. He offered a prize of twenty-five thousand dollars to whomever made the first nonstop flight from New York City to Paris, France.

As Lindbergh flew his lonely mail route with only the moon glistening from the frozen lakes to keep him company, he wondered about the Atlantic crossing. What kind of airplane would it take?

Commander Richard E. Byrd had a Fokker trimotor like the one he used for the first flight over the North Pole. The cost? Ninety thousand dollars for the airplane alone!

The French aviator René Fonch chose a biplane with three powerful air-cooled engines to make the Atlantic crossing. The American Legion entered a four-engine aircraft that cost more than one hundred thousand dollars.

Lindbergh realized that those people who knew of his decision to attempt the crossing believed that he didn't have much of a chance. He looked much too young to be a professional flier and, in fact, he had only four years of flying experience, and most of that was in battered army surplus airplanes.

Of all the fliers who decided to try to fly the Atlantic, he seemed the least likely to succeed. He didn't even own an airplane!

Lindbergh had saved only two thousand dollars, but he believed an airplane capable of crossing the Atlantic could be constructed for much less than most people believed.

Lindbergh convinced businessmen in Saint Louis to back his flight. He said he would need only ten thousand dollars to purchase a plane. "Engines drive up the cost of an airplane. I'll use only one engine."

Most people thought two or three engines made an airplane safer. Lindbergh disagreed. "Two engines double the chance of a failure. If one engine fails, the strain put upon the other engine would be too great."

Lindbergh explained, "I know the perfect engine for an airplane. The Wright Whirlwind is a new kind of engine with nine cylinders, air cooled, and it weighs only five hundred pounds." Best of all, recent tests showed that it ran for nine thousand hours between breakdowns.

Lindbergh discovered that Charles Levine of New York owned a Wright-Bellanca ready to fly.

Giuseppi Bellanca had developed the airplane especially for the Wright engine. Levine offered the airplane for sale.

Lindbergh had almost closed the deal when Levine said, "Of course, we'll select the crew."

Lindbergh stood speechless. Although he would own the airplane, he wouldn't be allowed to fly it!

Levine stood firm. A crash would give the plane a bad name. Lindbergh looked too young, too inexperienced as a pilot.

Lindbergh returned to Saint Louis by train. Time was running out, and he still didn't have an airplane.

Then from San Diego, California, Lindbergh received a wire from the Ryan Aircraft Company. Lindbergh visited San Diego and found the Ryan Company on the waterfront. The smell of fish was everywhere. The company, unknown and small, impressed Lindbergh because everyone was so friendly.

He talked with Donald Hall, the chief engineer. They figured out the best design. The airplane would have a single engine, and unlike the biplanes, a single overhead wing. Lindbergh wanted a gas tank in front, next to the motor.

"You will not be able to see forward," Hall pointed out.

"The engine blocks forward visibility anyway," Lindbergh said. "The pilot is safer if he is not trapped between the motor and gas tank."

Hall asked, "Where do you want the seat for your copilot?"

Lindbergh said, "I'll need only a single seat."

"You don't plan to make the flight alone?" Hall asked. That was an unthinkable idea. Admiral Byrd was taking a crew of four!

Lindbergh said, "Every pound of weight I save will mean another pound of gasoline."

He and Hall cut out every extra pound. Lindbergh's seat was a wicker chair. He eliminated lights for night landing and the gas gauges. Lindbergh decided to fly without a parachute and without a radio.

The Ryan factory finished the airplane within two months. Lindbergh flew to New York, with a stop in Saint Louis to show the plane to his partners. He named the plane *The Spirit of St. Louis.*

In New York, the weather had turned bad. Clouds, mud, and fog made flying dangerous. The Wright-Bellanca, the one Lindbergh had first tried to purchase, cracked up while landing.

Commander Byrd's huge three-engine Fokker crashed during a test flight, and the American Legion aircraft crashed and burned during a test flight over Virginia.

Two Frenchmen, Nungesser and Coli, successfully took off from Le Bourget Field north of Paris. They never landed in New York. Their plane, the *White Bird,* disappeared over the stormy Atlantic.

These experienced pilots failed. Could Lindbergh succeed? Newspapers called him the Lone Eagle. They didn't give him much chance for success.

Lindbergh continued to eliminate excess weight. He ripped spare pages from his notebook and cut parts from his charts that were not needed for the flight. Water and food? He took a quart of water, four sandwiches, and one hard boiled egg.

A stamp collector offered him one thousand dollars to fly a pound of letters to Paris. Lindbergh refused.

He and *The Spirit of St. Louis* were ready. On May

20, 1927, the rain stopped. At three o'clock in the morning Lindbergh drove to Roosevelt Field. The wet weather caused the engine to run roughly. Lindbergh climbed into the cramped cabin and closed the door.

He fixed his flying goggles. "Kick out the blocks."

The plane began slowly in the sticky mud. At the halfway point the wheels continued to cut deep marks in the mud. Lindbergh had to make the decision: either cut the engine or continue.

Lindbergh decided. Go! The controls answered. He gained lift. The wheels skipped once, twice, then pulled free.

Lindbergh did it. Thirty-three hours and thirty-nine minutes later 150,000 people waited for him at LaBourget Field. The gray white airplane cut through the darkness and bounced to a stop. The crowd crashed through the iron fence and surrounded the plane before the propellor stopped.

The flight made Charles Lindbergh a hero. The public accepted aviation with confidence for the first time. But more than that, Lindbergh showed that a man could accomplish any job to which he set his mind.

24

Moon Mad

On a cold March morning in 1926 Robert Hutchings Goddard set up a rocket in a field outside Worcester, Massachusetts. Snow covered the field, and the temperature didn't rise above freezing. But the sky was clear, and the wind didn't blow, and that was what mattered.

Robert Goddard lit the rocket with a blow torch. The flimsy contraption shot away from the frame which held it. The rocket flew to a landing two hundred feet away.

Although it was the first successful flight of a modern rocket, only a couple of Goddard's friends came to watch the flight. Goddard worked alone, except for his wife, Esther, who was always on hand. She took pictures of him standing by the little rocket. Later, her photographs were to be the only visual record of the first modern rocket flight.

Robert Goddard dreamed of a rocket to the moon and planets. It seemed like fantasy. Most people described him as being "moon mad."

Once, when he was a youngster, he climbed a tall cherry tree at the back of a barn on his grandfather's farm to trim dead branches. As he worked he thought about the chances of sending a rocket to the moon. This was four years *before* the Wright Brothers had made the first airplane flight at Kitty Hawk.

Robert looked into the problems of space travel, and he discovered that he would have to have considerably more knowledge if he were to be successful. He immediately began to study harder. He graduated from Worcester Polytechnic Institute at the top of his class.

He began building rocket motors in his laboratory and trying them out. He built a complete rocket in 1926. By then people learned he was interested in flights to the moon.

Professor A. W. Bickerton of England delivered an address to the British Association for the Advancement of Science. He described Goddard's work as a silly idea. "This foolish idea of shooting at the moon is an example of the absurd length to which vicious specialization will carry scientists working in thought-tight compartments. The proposition is basically impossible."

Robert Goddard continued his experiments. He constructed a larger rocket that carried a barometer, a thermometer, and a small camera to photograph the flight. It was the first rocket to carry a scientific "payload."

Unfortunately, the flight set a grass fire, and the farmers complained that the terrific roar from the engine disturbed their cows. The whole neighborhood complained and called the police.

Officials ordered Robert Goddard to put an end to his useless experiments. They forbade him to fire any more rockets in Massachusetts. Goddard stopped. He had run out of money for experiments anyway.

But Charles Lindbergh, who had become a national hero by his nonstop Atlantic crossing, visited Goddard. The rocket expert explained his ideas to Lindbergh. The famous aviator was quick to see the importance of the work. Lindbergh arranged for Goddard to receive fifty thousand dollars.

Robert Goddard and Esther immediately moved to Roswell, New Mexico, where they built a miniature space center—complete with a permanent launching tower.

Even while he worked to make rockets that would travel a couple of miles he drew pictures in his notebooks of rockets looping around the moon.

An editorial in the *New York Times* gleefully pointed out that a rocket motor wouldn't operate in the emptiness of space. "A Severe Strain on Credulity," was the title of the editorial, and it went on to say, "The motor would have nothing to push against." And about Goddard the newspaper said, "He doesn't know the relation of action to reaction. He lacks the knowledge ladled out daily in high school."

Could a rocket operate in the vacuum of space? Robert Goddard had long ago settled that problem. While still in college he pumped air out of a long pipe, and fired a small rocket motor inside. The engine *did* work in a vacuum.

The real problems of space flight, Goddard knew, were cooling the combustion chamber and steering the rocket in a straight path as it flew.

As the liquid oxygen and kerosene burned, the flame became so hot it soon melted any metal. Scientists knew of no metal which could withstand the intense heat. Goddard solved this by running fuel lines around the back side of the combustion chamber. The fuel spiraled several times around the chamber as it flowed into the engine. The fuel cooled the metal and kept it from melting.

To steer the rocket, Goddard used a gyroscope. This small spinning top revolves in a cage. The gyroscope, when it is spinning rapidly, automatically resists any force that tries to change its position.

Still, no one thought space travel possible.

Canadian astronomer Professor J. W. Campbell

of the University of Alberta said, "Rocket flight would appear to be more than one hundred years in the future. The finished rocket would need to weigh a million tons to carry one pound to the moon."

Richard Van der Riet Woolley, England's highest-ranking scientist, said, "It must be said at once that the whole procedure presents difficulties of so fundamental a nature that we are forced to dismiss the notion as essentially impractical."

The American government never became interested in Goddard's work, although the famous German V-2 rocket proved his ideas were correct. The V-2 was based upon many of the 214 patents which Goddard received for his rocket work.

Dr. Vannevar Bush, who helped develop analog calculators and ran the nuclear energy program after World War II, testified before a Senate Committee, "The people have been talking about a three-thousand-mile high-angle rocket shot from one continent to another. In my opinion such a thing is impossible for many years."

Of course, famous scientists couldn't stop the rocket with words. Only forty years after Goddard launched his four-foot-high rocket in the Massachusetts field, a Saturn Five blasted off for the moon!

Edwin Aldrin (everyone called him Buzz) flew aboard that Saturn V which headed for the moon. Once before he had been in space, aboard Gemini 12. At that time he made a space walk and carried with him a prayer written by his nurse: "The light of God surrounds me; the love of God enfolds me; the power of God protects me; the presence of God watches over me; wherever I am, God is."

The Gemini program was finished. Now Buzz Aldrin, Mike Collins, and Neil Armstrong were on their way—on their way to the moon!

Each astronaut had packed a small white bag with personal things to take to the moon and return to earth. Buzz Aldrin transferred the two white bags from the locker under Mike Collins's couch and stowed them in the spidery Eagle, the moon ship.

The Eagle's footpads touched dust—moon-dust—at 21:18 GMT (3:18 CST) on Sunday afternoon, July 20, 1969. Armstrong cut the engine.

"Houston, Tranquility Base here," Armstrong said, his voice came clear and calm. Then with triumph, he said, "The Eagle has landed!"

The two astronauts immediately began powering down the ship to conserve energy. Buzz finished his part of the power down. Then he removed four small objects from his personal preference kit: a little silver cup, a small plastic container of wine, a small piece of bread, and a sheet of paper with a Scripture verse written on it. Buzz laid the objects on the flat top of the computer.

He spoke to Houston. "I'd like everyone listening in to pause a moment to contemplate the events of the past few hours and give thanks in his or her own way."

The people at Houston respected his request for radio silence. Buzz quickly prepared for his special Communion. He had saved the bread and wine from a Communion service taken with friends a week before at a church outside Houston.

The wine poured in slow motion because of the one-sixth gravity on the moon. Buzz unfolded the tiny sheet of paper. As he took the Communion, he read the verse of Scripture: "I am the vine, ye are the branches. . . ."

It seemed altogether fitting to Buzz that the first act of men on the moon should be an act of religious faith.

25

Impossible—That's All!

During the first century A.D. the Roman engineer Julius Frontinus wrote a book in which he said no more important inventions were possible, and "for their improvement I see no further hope in applied arts."

Last century in the United States, the director of the Patent Office thought the office should be closed. He believed that there would be no more important inventions.

Impossible ideas have a way of becoming history. A student of history says, "If a great scientist says something is possible, then it usually is. But if he says it is not possible, then he is probably wrong."

When Samuel Morse first proposed the idea of sending messages through wires by the use of an electric current, many people believed this both impossible and useless.

In 1842, Morse scraped together enough money to demonstrate his telegraph in Washington. He sent messages from one committee room to another. He had already sold the invention in Europe, but the money from congress to help him establish a telegraph line barely passed. Congressman David Wallace, who voted for the telegraph line from Washington to Baltimore, lost the next election because his opponent charged that he had wasted the people's money in such a silly project.

Steamships and ocean liners? Impossible! In 1820, Joseph Henry of the United States visited England and spoke before the British Association for the Advancement of Science in Liverpool. He told of American steamships which reached the speed of fifteen knots.

Joseph Henry also reported that he believed steamships would soon be able to make the voyage directly from New York to Liverpool across the Atlantic under steam.

An English scientist named Dionysius Larder stood to speak, and he accused Henry of exaggeration. First, he said that Henry must be mistaken. Steamships could never reach the speed of fifteen knots.

And as for crossing the Atlantic, Dr. Larder ended with these words, "A voyage directly from New York to Liverpool under steam is, I have no hesitation in saying, wildly fanciful, and he might as well talk of making a voyage from New York to the moon."

Gravity waves? Impossible! Einstein thought gravity traveled through space in the form of waves, similar to light waves, but he believed gravity waves would be impossible to detect because they would be too weak.

In 1969, Dr. Joseph Weber, professor of physics at the University of Maryland, announced his detection of gravity waves. Other scientists greeted his reports with skepticism and personal attacks. He must be mistaken! Gravity waves were impossible to detect.

Three years later other scientists succeeded in detecting gravity waves. Gravity waves turned out to be ten thousand times stronger than Einstein thought they would be! The criticism of Dr. Weber has subsided and many scientists wish they had not dismissed his announcement so quickly.

If Dr. Weber had not performed the experiment in the first place, then years might have passed before the truth about gravity waves became known.

Something like this happened in the field of chemistry. The inert gases—helium, neon, argon, krypton, xenon, and radon—are noted because of their lack of chemical activity. Chemistry teachers used to say there was no reason to study the inert gases. They have an electron structure which makes it impossible for them to form compounds with other elements.

Inert, in fact, means "no action." The inert gases remained alone and aloof. This is what chemistry textbooks said. It had been said for so long no one thought to doubt the textbooks.

Then, about ten years ago, Neil Bartlett, a chemist at the University of British Columbia in Canada, wondered if it were true. He could find no record of experiments which backed up the statement.

Neil Bartlett chose to investigate xenon. He heated a mixture of xenon gas and fluorine gas inside a can made of nickel metal.

He chose fluorine because it is the most reactive element, even more reactive than oxygen, which will react with almost anything. Fluorine has to be handled carefully. One whiff of fluorine would be a whiff of death. The metal nickel has been known for years by chemists as a catalyst. A catalyst helps speed up reactions. Heat supplies energy to make a chemical reaction begin.

In other words, Neil Bartlett chose the most logical experiment to force xenon to form a chemical compound.

When Neil Bartlett concluded his experiment, he found a tiny purple crystal made of xenon and fluorine. Chemists shook their heads in disbelief. Xenon *did* react with other elements.

Soon crystals were produced of the other inert

gases. Of course, the inert gases could no longer be called by that name. Instead, the term *noble gases* is used.

Compounds of inert gases, gravity waves, rocket ships and moon flights, ocean liners and steamships, trains and transcontinental railroads, telegraphs and telephones, suspension bridges and underwater tunnels; all of these have faced determined opposition by people who thought such ideas were impossible.

What about the miracles in the Bible? Are they impossible? Dr. William F. Nolen, who wrote the book *The Making of a Surgeon,* disagrees. He says, "Miracles do occur." One of his patients was a young boy who had a large tumor in the abdomen. Dr. Nolen told the parents there was nothing he could do. The boy was beyond the help of doctors. "His life is in the hands of the Lord." The boy made a simple, uneventful recovery. Five years later he was alive and well without a trace of the tumor.

Impossible? No! Jesus says, "With men it is impossible, but not with God; for with God all things are possible."

26

Ancient Men, Modern Minds

In the past, and even up until this present moment, leading experts had the tendency as they grew older to let their opinions harden into prejudices. They presented their theories as absolute facts with a take-it-or-else attitude that discouraged questions.

The French prehistorian Breuil is an example. He was jealous of his own ideas about the origins of man. At meetings he shouted down younger scientists who disagreed with him. One of his students said, "The older he became the more difficult it became personally to disagree with him."

It is not surprising, then, to find that information which disagrees with deeply entrenched theories, such as the theory of evolution, is seldom voiced at scientific meetings. Few young scientists are willing to suffer the ridicule they would receive by voicing their doubts.

Few people understand the difficult path a new discovery must follow before it is presented to the scientific community. Before a scientist can even begin a new investigation, he must have permission from his program director. But the program director is an "expert" who will think twice before giving permission to the young scientist to set off on what will be, as the director sees it, a wild goose chase.

Without the director's approval, the young scientist will receive no money to begin his work. Seldom is a scientist wealthy enough to finance his own investigation. Instead, money for such work must come from a university or foundation.

But a final hurdle remains after the work is finished. The discovery must be printed in a scholarly journal. The investigator will not receive credit otherwise, and the new discovery will remain unknown to other scientists.

This is not a simple matter. Scientific journals have space for only a small percentage of the papers they receive. Each manuscript is read by a committee of experts before it is published. If the paper appears to contradict established scientific ideas, then it may be returned to the investigator.

Amateurs have an especially difficult time breaking into print in scientific journals. We have seen in previous chapters the delay that Mendel's paper on pea plants suffered, and the difficulty that Fraunhofer encountered in appearing before scientific meetings to tell about the lines in the sun's spectrum.

This attitude has hurt science. Amateurs do make important discoveries. Medicine suffered because doctors failed to recognize the importance of bacteria discovered by Leeuwenhoek. Air flight owes its greatest debt to the Wright brothers. Another amateur, Paul Emile Botta, showed archaeologists how the Bible could be used to uncover lost cities.

When it comes to new findings that contradict the theory of evolution, the amateur has an even more difficult time. Don Marcelino de Sautuola, a nobleman and amateur archaeologist, found this out when he began working in a cave called Altamira near his estate in Spain. The year was 1879, two decades after Darwin announced his theory of evolution.

Scientists who believe evolution discount the

achievements of ancient people. For evolution to work there must be a step-by-step change of primitive living things into more complex living things. For this to be true, the mind of ancient man must be judged inferior to the mind of modern man.

For four years Don Marcelino worked off and on in the cave. He found bits of bone and shell—and ashes from an ancient fire—that proved the cave had been occupied by human beings a long time ago.

During the summer, Maria, Don Marcelino's daughter, asked to go with him into the cave. While he dug around on the cavern floor, she studied the ceiling by candle light. Suddenly she called to her father, "Papa! Come look! Painted bulls!"

Don Marcelino looked up to where she pointed. In the flickering light of the girl's candle, he stared in amazement at spectacular drawings of painted animals thundering across the ceiling.

Don Marcelino had never thought to look overhead. He had spent all of his time digging around on the floor for scraps of bones.

The paintings took his breath away. Animals appeared to move as if they were alive. Bison grazed, wild horses pranced, and angry bulls charged. Why did they seem so alive? Don Marcelino realized the artist had used the bulges and hollows in the rocky roof to form rippling muscles. The animals looked three dimensional.

The graceful bison could have been the work of an artist as skilled as Rembrandt or Michelangelo. One Spanish artist said, "Their execution shows no sign of primitive art."

Don Marcelino had enough money to publish a book describing the paintings. He included in the book sketches of the animals. The experts who read the book could not accept his discovery. "A hoax!" they cried. "Primitive man was a barbarian and hardly more than an ape."

Could beautiful animals such as these be the work of dim-witted cave people?

The cave paintings indicated ancient man had great artistic ability. But to admit this would be to admit progress in reverse. Those who believed in the steady upward climb of mankind were shaken and angered by Don Marcelino's book.

Emile Cartailhac, the leading professor of prehistory in France, denounced the paintings as frauds without even bothering to make the trip from France to Spain to view them in person, although Don Marcelino offered to pay the professor's travel expenses.

In 1883, Don Marcelino appeared before a conference on prehistory. He showed the professors lumps of pigment. He passed around clam shells the ancient artist had used to hold the paint. He demonstrated how the artist had ground iron oxide and mixed it with animal fat to make oil paint in colors varying from yellow to dark orange and brown. Black pigment was made from charred bones.

Yet because Emile Cartailhac led the opposition, the conference decided that the paintings were the work of a modern painter.

This was a dishonest decision because the same dating method that gave the age of the bones also gave the age of the paintings. They both were the same age. If ancient man had lived in the cave, then ancient man had created the vivid animals charging across the ceiling.

Three years later another conference met. The professors refused to let Don Marcelino—an amateur—appear before them. No scientific publication accepted his paper about the Altamira cave paintings.

The matter stood suspended in disbelief for sixteen years. Then, in France, a second cave was opened. The entrance had been sealed for centuries. Inside, explorers found more cave art. It was as vigorous and as powerful as any paintings in a Paris museum.

This time even Professor Cartailhac admitted he had been wrong. He apologized in a book called *Confessions of a Skeptic.* He traveled to Spain, but Don Marcelino had long since died. The professor apologized to Maria instead. "It is I, and not your father, who have been foolish."

The lesson of the cave at Altamira was difficult for prehistorians to take. The paintings challenged their fondest assumption—the evolution of man. This was the reason why it took more than twenty years for the scientific world to accept the paintings as genuine.

Most of the caves have been closed to the public. Scientists are anxious to preserve the paintings until new tools and new methods have been developed to answer more questions about the brown and gold animals on the ceiling.

But there is a danger in closing the cave. A visitor may notice something a trained scientist might miss. After all, twelve-year-old Maria discovered the animals her well-educated father had missed for four years!

Also a student of science who is trained in one field is not welcome when he "intrudes" upon another man's territory. Doctors didn't welcome Pasteur when he switched from chemistry to medicine. The same sort of thing happened to Harvey H. Nininger who had been trained as a geologist. When he began collecting meteorites he got very little help from professional astronomers.

A person will find what he expects to find and overlook what he thinks cannot occur. Dr. Arthur Smith Woodward and Sir Arthur Keith wanted desperately to find fossil remains of a man-ape. When they uncovered the Piltdown hoax, they rushed to accept the discovery.

Prehistorians are no different. Their minds have been steeped in years of study—they know what to expect. New ideas must fit within their body of knowledge. The Altamira cave paintings didn't fit, so the paintings were rejected.

Ancient man had every bit as much imagination and intelligence as we have today. For the first time in a hundred years, scientists who doubt evolution are willing to put their doubts into words. They have begun to offer solid scientific evidence that refutes the view that man developed from lower creatures.

Sir John Eccles, the Australian physiologist who won the Nobel Prize in physiology in 1963, contends that man is such an enormously complex organism, that intelligent life could not originate twice in the same universe.

A basic law of physical science states that things naturally change from a state of organization to a state of disorganization. In everyday experience we see this. Everything tends to wear out, to grow old, to run down, to crumble, and to become more disorganized.

This is a strange situation! In physical science, things are observed to go from a more ordered to a less ordered condition. In life science, however, the assumption is reversed. Living things are thought to become more organized.

Another basic assumption of evolution concerns how life began. Without a creator, life had to begin somewhere; and the evolutionists assume that life began as tiny one-celled animals in the sea. Somehow, they say, the chemicals of life got together and set the chain of evolution into motion.

Francis Crick, who won the Nobel Prize for unraveling the DNA molecule that carries the secret of heredity, doubts whether life began in a primeval sea.

The first one-celled animals in the primeval sea would have had to use the chemicals around it to begin the process of life. But Francis Crick points out that molybdenum, which is an important chemical of life, is relatively rare in sea water and that nickel and chromium, which are more abundant, would have served in the same chemical reactions as molybdenum.

Crick also finds it strange that all life on earth is controlled by a single genetic code. Such an idea leaves many molecular biologists feeling, as Crick puts it, "slightly uncomfortable."

It is fitting that this book should end with the topic of evolution. Because here—and nowhere else—is the choice so clear cut. Biologists say that man is nothing more than an advanced animal who evolved from lesser animals. The Bible clearly teaches that man is created by God, and is not an animal at all. The psalmist said, "And yet you [God] have made him [man] only a little lower than the angels, and placed a crown of glory and honor upon his head" (Ps. 8:5, The Living Bible). This verse must be important because it is repeated in Hebrews, and therefore it is one of the few verses found in both the Old and New Testaments.

Which is true? Which is false? If the choice is between the Bible and science, then which one can fail? Joshua said, "But as for me and my family, we will serve the Lord."